ADVENTURES OF A
Grenfell Nurse

ADVENTURES OF A
Grenfell Nurse

1952–1954

ROSALIE M. LOMBARD

Library of Congress Control Number:		2014919706
ISBN:	Hardcover	978-1-5035-1302-0
	Softcover	978-1-5035-1303-7
	eBook	978-1-5035-1304-4

This book was printed in the United States of America.

Rev. date: 11/06/2014

To order additional copies of this book, contact:
Xlibris
1-888-795-4274
www.Xlibris.com
Orders@Xlibris.com
669350

CONTENTS

In memory of Dr. Gordon W. Thomas

1919–1996

Introduction

The Seed is Planted

Like other children of the 1930s, I read about the adventures of Sir Wilfred Grenfell who worked among fishermen in a very cold, icy place way up north called Newfoundland and Labrador. I still have my copy of his book, *Forty Years for Labrador*, that was published in 1932 with the memorable story, "Adrift on an Icepan." To me, at that young age, it was exciting stuff, but it soon became buried somewhere in my subconscious. Another reminder of that esteemed man happened as a result of my stamp-collecting hobby that was begun at age twelve. In 1941, a beautiful, eye-catching blue Newfoundland stamp was issued with a picture of Sir Wilfred looking off in the distance toward his medical service vessel *Maraval* from the bridge of the hospital ship *Strathcona II*. The seed was germinating.

It was many years later, during my student-nursing days at Columbia-Presbyterian, that I really learned what the Grenfell Mission was all about. Our junior class (as per tradition) was assigned to devise and carry out a bazaar from which the proceeds would be given to a worthy cause of our choice. Our dean had known nurses and doctors who had served in an organization called the Grenfell Mission. She casually dropped this name as one we might want to consider, and after some research, we did decide to have it be our recipient. The bazaar was a great success, netting $1,800, and it was my privilege, as a class officer, to deliver the check to the secretary of the New York branch of the International Grenfell Association (as it was then titled). I could easily detect that she was enthusiastic about her job and the work being done in Newfoundland. She told me about the people and showed me slides of Dr. Thomas on his medical rounds in the community. I was intrigued at the thought of, someday, using *my* nursing skills there and added this information to my memory bank.

After graduating in 1951, I remained at the medical center for another year of nursing experience. In that time, I had got tired of the large city and yearned for a more adventurous working environment. Those earlier seeds about the Grenfell persona had sprouted. In the summer of 1952, I met again with the IGA secretary and signed up for one year as an Assistant Nurse in St. Anthony. The seed that had been planted so many years before had finally blossomed and would lead me to great adventures.

Part I

The Setting

Sir Wilfred Grenfell founded the Grenfell Mission in northern Newfoundland and Labrador in 1892 as a medical service to the people in that isolated part of Canada. As late as my own time there (1952–1954), no roads connected that area to the southern part of the province. In addition to the Newfoundlanders, many Inuit (Eskimo) and Innu (Indian) patients came down from "The Labrador" for medical care. The primary means of transportation was by boat in the summer and dogsled in the winter. Air travel for patient care was still in its infancy. One lone caterpillar-traction snowmobile had arrived for the purpose of transporting huge cans of milk from the mission dairy barn to the hospital.

My *applicant's information* brochure contained, among other things, the following items:

> The climate is rugged and variable. During the long winters the harbours are frozen and there is deep snow. In the coastal regions, winters are severe, there is considerable fog in summer, but the weather is bracing, with some warm days. Up the bays, the climate is

dryer and somewhat milder, and summer days can be occasionally quite warm.

Living conditions are comfortable at all Grenfell stations. Diet is adequate, though not varied.

Hospitals: St. Anthony, 80 beds, 2 annexes, 44 beds; North West River, 17 beds; Harrington, 21 beds; Cartwright, 20 beds.

Nursing Stations: Mutton Bay, Forteau, St. Mary's River, Spotted Islands (summer), Flowers Cove, and Canada Bay.

Ships: *Maraval*, a 75 ft. hospital ship traveling the area in summer; *Nellie A. Cluett,* a 134 ft. freighter supplying all stations from Canadian ports.

Annual Starting Salaries: Medical doctor in charge—$2,500, travel and board, depending on experience; Nurse in charge of Station—$900, travel and board ($1,050 at St. Anthony); Assistant Nurses—$750, travel and board.

The work, covering approximately 1200 miles, is divided into 4 medical districts. Hospitals are located at key points, with nursing stations interspersed at isolated places.

After an interview in the New York office in the summer of 1952, I was accepted as an Assistant Nurse at the main hospital in St. Anthony, Newfoundland. I set out for this new experience in October 1952, traveling by train from Boston to North Sydney, Nova Scotia, crossing on the overnight steamer *Cabot Strait* to Port aux Basques, Newfoundland. Then I boarded the railroad with the expectation of later being bussed to Hampden from where the hospital ship, *Maraval*, would travel the remaining four hundred miles north to St. Anthony. However, a monkey wrench was thrown into the schedule when we were train wrecked at St. Teresa, a remote place near Flat Bay Ballast Pit, Newfoundland.

Eventually, I did arrive in St. Anthony where I remained for two of the most exciting and interesting years of my life. The experiences in nursing were a far cry from those I had had at the Columbia-Presbyterian Medical Center in New York City. I loved the challenges presented by having to make do with (or improve) scanty or obsolete equipment and working with barebones staffing. I enjoyed the contact with fellow workers and patients from other cultures and dealing with the elements, whether sailing on the ocean or traveling by dog team. I believe that this Grenfell experience enhanced my global awareness and contributed to my desire in later years for more foreign travel. Those years spent in that isolated environment, when the Grenfell spirit still existed, certainly enriched my life.

Part II

The Journey

1 Northward Bound

In September of 1952, it was difficult to say good-bye to my three best buddies and the apartment we had happily shared since our graduation from Columbia-Presbyterian department of nursing. It had been a wonderful living situation, close to the medical center, but more importantly, it was a harmonious, positive blending of four different personalities.

I headed north to my hometown, Keene, New Hampshire, to spend the next few weeks with family and to make preparations for my new assignment. How exciting it was, at the age of twenty-five, to contemplate the new adventure at this eighty-bed hospital in St. Anthony, Newfoundland, located on the subarctic northernmost coastal rim of the island.

As I packed my trunk and gear, I followed the suggested list for clothing and equipment: "heavy coat, sweaters, wool skirts, scarves, ski pants, uniforms, wool underwear, fly and mosquito preventive, flashlight and camera. Electrical equipment is not advised because of power shortage and high voltage."

These items were supplemented by my own perceived essentials: skis, ski poles, boots, technical books, battery-operated radio and lantern, movie camera, movie projector, and a .22-caliber rifle. (I cannot now imagine why on earth I decided to take the rifle or how I dared to do so.)

The days leading up to my departure were touched with excitement as well as a certain anxiety, not due only to my unfamiliarity with my prospective situation, but to the fact that the mission instructions were constantly changing. One day, I got a letter advising me to leave "next Friday from Boston," and later the same day, another arrived saying "leave on Tuesday." Then a telegram came with instructions to disregard both letters. On Sunday, a final telegram stated that I was to leave on Tuesday after all.

On that warm, pleasant New England Tuesday, October 14, 1952, I boarded the 9:30 PM train in Boston—along with my carefully packed trunk, movie projector and small suitcase, skis and poles—for the first leg of my journey into an unfamiliar territory. It was my first experience of spending nights on a train. Even the thought of occupying a berth in the Pullman car and eating in the diner added to my sense of adventure.

The crisp clickety-clack of the rails made sleep fitful; besides, my head was full of worries about the cold and the isolation of the place where I was going. *Have I packed the proper clothing and equipment? Will my nursing skills and stamina be sufficient for what lies ahead?*

Arriving in Truro, Nova Scotia, the following evening, I changed to the train to North Sydney. I trusted that my trunk and gear also made the change. I knew that another Grenfell worker, named Marilyn Tolley, was heading for St. Anthony also. Sure enough, when morning finally arrived, I bumped into someone who fit my idea of a new Vassar College graduate: a young, attractive woman with curly auburn hair nattily clad in a tailored, burnt-orange coat with scarf and binoculars slung over her shoulder. I enthusiastically inquired "Are you Tolley?" just as she blurted out "Are you Lombard?" From that first exchange, we became friends and shared many adventures over the ensuing two years.

With a new traveling companion, the trip became much more enjoyable. We hurriedly got off the train at 7:00 AM in North Sydney, eager to check out our new surroundings. Since we were not scheduled to depart until 8:30 PM, we had the whole day to explore the area.

We found a taxi (the only one in town) and the driver took us to the Hotel New Belmont for a whopping seventy-five cents each—which struck us as expensive when we discovered that the hotel was only two blocks away. We rented a room for the day, and each took a delicious hot bath to soothe the travel-worn body. We stowed our luggage and set out on foot in the pouring rain to check out the town.

A nearby pond was the habitat of two beautiful mute swans. I christened my new movie camera by recording them as they flew back and forth, gliding gracefully to the surface of the water again.

A mile or so further on, we reached the highest point of land, overlooking the harbour, and where fishing boats of various sizes were moored. For the first time, we caught sight of the much larger coastal steamer that would carry us across the one hundred-mile expanse to Port aux Basques, Newfoundland. We headed toward the ship. Soon we read *Cabot Strait* on her bow and witnessed a flurry of activity. We watched the meticulous loading of baggage, supplies, and animals including many horses, while crewmen used all kinds of interesting slings, pulleys, and cranes to accomplish the task. This seemed to go on endlessly, but finally, we saw our own trunks go into the hold, and we felt relieved and left.

We returned to the hotel (capacity of ten rooms or less), gathered our luggage, checked out at the desk, and made our way back to the ship. We certainly didn't want to miss our departure time of 8:30 PM. We boarded, found our cabin, and became acquainted with the various facilities on the ship. The gangplank was finally lifted at 11:30 PM, and the *Cabot Strait* inched its way out of the harbour. We had just been introduced to the flexibility of transportation schedules in the Maritimes.

Most of that night, we endured the mighty rolling of the ship from our cabin bunks. Finally, we could no longer ignore the queasiness in our stomachs and fled to the upper deck for some air and were refreshed by the salt breeze on our faces. We moved to the windward deck, searching the pitch-black night in vain for a glimpse of land. We were drenched by a huge wave breaking over the rail as a reminder from the sea that she—not the land—was still in charge. We soon retreated to the comfort of our cabin to dry off and make ready for disembarkation.

A couple of hours later, we made our way up through the hatchway and returned to the deck. Dawn had broken, seas were calmer, and we were excited to finally see in the distance our "New Founde Land," as it had been dubbed centuries before by other seafarers, where we would soon be planting our feet.

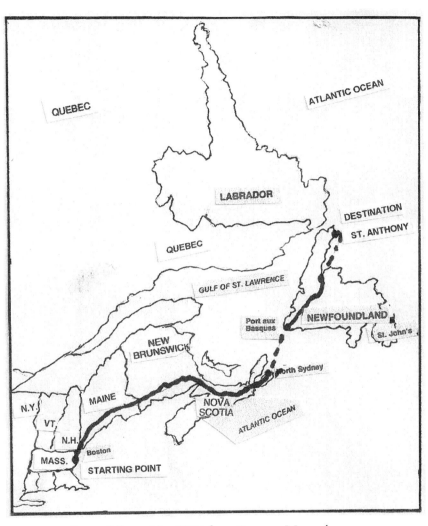

*Route followed in 1952 from Boston, Massachusetts,
to St. Anthony, Newfoundland*

2 Arriving on Newfoundland Soil

We watched with keen interest as the crew and dockhands lashed the *Cabot Strait* to the pier. As soon as the gangplank was in place, Marilyn and I were the first passengers to disembark, anxious to explore the town of Port aux Basques, our first encounter with Newfoundland.

SS Cabot Strait
(Courtesy of Railway Coastal Museum, St. John's)

As our sea legs adjusted to terra firma, we searched for a nearby restaurant or diner to satisfy our hunger pangs. We walked and walked through the bleak town, not daring to wander too far because we were already late for the train's scheduled 9:30 AM departure.

Finally we saw Harry's Restaurant and ran toward it only to be greeted by a *Closed* sign on the door. As we started to leave, our hopes were raised at the sight of a Chinese fellow on a bicycle, heading straight for the restaurant. He jangled his keys as he opened the front door and turned the cardboard sign to read *Open*. In a flash, he fired up the stove and served us a hearty, most welcome breakfast.

No sooner had we eaten than we heard the unmistakable whistle of a train and ran to the distant station for the next leg of our journey. We learned that we would be boarding the *Newfie Bullet*, as it was affectionately known. It was a railroad system spanning the 907 kilometers (564 miles) between Port aux Basques and the capital, St. John's, utilizing a single set of narrow gauge tracks (except for occasional sidings). We were told by one of the Newfoundlanders that he had heard that a passenger could get off the first car while the train is moving, pick a quart of berries, then hop back on the last car to continue his journey.

We pulled out of the Port aux Basques station at about 10:30 AM, already several hours late. If we had realized that the train would never depart until all the cargo was transferred from the *Cabot Strait*, we would have been much more relaxed.

We read the quaint names of the outpost towns as we moved along at thirty to thirty-five miles per hour—Come By Chance, Flat Bay Ballast Pit, Tickle Harbour, Hodgewater, St. Teresa—ah, Saint Teresa! We suddenly felt a series of major jolts and heard crashing and screeching up ahead. We were certain we were falling off a bridge or something worse, but suddenly, we came to a halt on a wicked slant. An elderly Newfoundlander sitting nearby looked out the window and calmly stated, "I b'leve we be off the tracks." We all clambered from our seats and down the steps to see what on earth had happened. Our car (number 45) was off the tracks, but everything ahead of ours was in an even bigger mess. *We had been wrecked!* Engine number 307, belching steam and wheels still spinning, lay over the embankment upside down. The rest of the cars were accordion-pleated, the iron rails coiled and twisted—no doubt in agony after having been straight as arrows for all those many years since 1891.

Overturned Engine no. 307 (RML)

Fireman in Engine no. 307 Train Wreck (RML)

Engineer of Engine no. 307 in Train Wreck (RML)

Marilyn Tolley and Overturned Engine no. 307 (RML)

Undercarriage of Engine no. 307 (RML)

Passengers wandered along the precarious edge of the railroad bed to survey the wreckage. I was engrossed in recording the entire scene with my new movie camera, including the dramatic sight of the engineer and fireman emerging from the overturned engine and being helped up the embankment by other crewmen. The engineer's face was covered with blood, and the steam had burned both men. I had been so completely wrapped up in my photographic endeavors that it never occurred to me until this whole episode was over that I was the only person on the train with any formal medical training. Fortunately, there were two older women who cared for the injured men. I reassured myself by rationalizing that their grueling life experiences probably made them more competent than I to handle the situation.

It didn't escape our attention, of course, that there was only one set of railroad tracks and those badly mangled. We wondered how we would ever get on with our journey from this place in the middle of nowhere. There were no houses and no curious onlookers other than the passengers. We learned later that the crew was only able to communicate with the railroad dispatch office by climbing the telegraph pole and "cutting in" to the wires strung along the tracks.

Newfoundlanders, who were acquainted with the *Newfie Bullet*, speculated that sudden frigid temperatures had caused frost heaves that separated the tracks enough to topple the unstable engine. The next few cars followed along with the baggage car containing our trunks and equipment. (Our baggage arrived in St. Anthony six weeks later on the coastal steamer.)

We knew we were in for a substantial delay, and along with all the Newfoundlanders, we relaxed. Marilyn played her guitar, and many joined in the singing even if the tunes were unfamiliar. Soon, several decks of cards appeared, and various games were started. We never once heard anyone complain or say "I'm supposed to be at an important meeting," or "My family will be worried sick," or "Should we sue the railroad?" No, these people knew that whenever transportation is involved (in this part of the world), the weather rules supremely, and one must be prepared for anything. We *too* were learning this lesson. Occasionally, as the train sat idle, we did hear such quips as "Moy, this be a smooth ride," or "I wonder where we is to now?"

Five hours after the incident occurred, several small, hand-operated rail repair cars arrived with men who surveyed the situation, enjoyed free meals in the dining car, and then returned from whence they came, having determined that they could do nothing until the next day. A small cabin car appeared on the rails about two hours later to take the two crewmen for medical care back to Port aux Basques in the pitch-black night. By this time, the cars were chilly and dimly lit (one light per car), so after taking advantage of the free meal in the dining car, everyone settled down to try to sleep. There seemed to be no information available about the next move, but no one, including Marilyn and myself, seemed concerned. We had begun to acquire the relaxed demeanor of the Newfies.

At 2:00 AM, when almost everyone in our car had fallen asleep, we heard a train coming down the tracks from the north. We learned that that train would exchange passengers with one soon to arrive from the south (at the rear of our train); then each would return to its respective station by traveling in reverse. Both groups of passengers headed for the appropriate car by walking along the ridge of the steep embankment— some going north and some south—all in the swirling snow, by the eerie light of one or two flares and a searchlight.

By noon, and heading north, our new cabin car was approaching Deer Lake, 173 miles from Port aux Basques. Our instructions had stated that Dr. Gordon Thomas, medical director at St. Anthony, would meet us there and would handle the remaining travel arrangements. Deer Lake was the last stop before heading directly north. No roads connected this area to the Upper Peninsula, so it would be necessary to travel the last four hundred miles by boat. We were more than twenty-four hours behind schedule with no means of communicating with Dr. Thomas or headquarters. Would he be aware that we were on *this* train, with a good excuse for being twenty-four hours late, or even that we had arrived in Newfoundland? We peered anxiously through the windows for some sign that we had not been abandoned.

As we detrained in Deer Lake, we immediately saw a young, handsome, well-dressed man standing nearby. I thought, *Could Dr. Thomas, medical director of the entire Grenfell Mission, be that young?* We soon had the answer as he quickly approached us. Apparently, we fit the descriptions of the women he was expecting to meet. He introduced himself and his wife and then seemed anxious for us all to be on our way. We naively said that we needed to wait for our baggage, but he said, in a firm voice, "There is no time for that," and we left immediately by taxi for our next stop. Already we could tell that he was a "take charge" kind of person, and we were more than willing to follow his instructions. We didn't realize that our trunks were still in the derailed baggage car back at St. Teresa. Six long weeks would elapse before we would see them again.

We sped along the fifty- to sixty-mile stretch of the bumpy, unpaved road to Hampden in a rickety taxi and were glad when we spotted the ocean in the distance and a ship tied up to the pier. I detected a bit of annoyance in Dr. Thomas's voice when he explained that the mission's hospital ship, the *Maraval*, had been waiting there for us for *two days*. At 2:00 PM, we had no sooner hit the deck than the crew pulled up the gangplank; the ship's whistle blew, and we were off.

MV *Maraval, the Travelling Clinic*
(Courtesy of "Among the Deep Sea Fishers," July 1959)

The *Maraval*, a seventy-five-foot ship with a diesel engine, was built to sail to the outposts along the coasts of Newfoundland and Labrador as a traveling clinic and to transport patients to the hospital at St. Anthony when necessary.

We checked out all the facilities on this ship that would be our home for the next two days; soon after, we were called to supper. It consisted of corned beef, cabbage, hard tack, and an atrocious mixture of lemon and water to drink. It was prepared by a rather grumpy cook, who admonished us to "show up early for breakfast."

We sailed about seventy miles along the rugged, rocky, uninhabited coast and moored at Harbour Deep for the night. We slept comfortably in the dispensary until 2:00 AM when it was time to find the "head." The trek to the aft part of the deck and down the hatch was snowy and downright chilly.

After our early breakfast, we sailed along smoothly until the last forty-five minutes of the trip when we crossed Hare Bay. The sea was rough and the waves broke over the deck. When we returned to the dispensary to pack, we found our suitcases (that we had left open), rolling back and forth across the floor with some of the contents strewn around and very wet.

We finally reached the landlocked harbour of St. Anthony, and soon the captain blew the whistle. Motoring in, we saw neat houses, fishing stages, and numerous moored boats. In the distance, we could see the mission buildings with which we would later become very familiar. We tied up to the wharf at about 4:00 PM where dozens of people, including most of the hospital staff and curious onlookers, already had gathered. We had arrived at our final destination after five days of travel, anxious to meet the staff and were looking forward to whatever adventures were in store.

Part III

The Destination

1—St. Anthony at Last

Finally reaching my destination, after five days of exciting travel, I was eager to meet the new challenges. I lost little time before exploring the new environment. My traveling companion, Marilyn, was whisked off to her new post at the orphanage, and Phyllis Baird, head nurse, escorted me to the hospital. My windowless room on the third floor was decorated simply—a straight chair, small bed, and chest of drawers—but adequate for the small number of hours to be spent there. The most glaring lack was my trunk, which I had so carefully packed and the contents of which I had previously deemed to be absolutely essential. I learned how foolish that assessment was during the next six weeks as I daily awaited its arrival and found that I could make do just fine without it.

The blazing fireplace in the first floor living room provided a warm introduction to the area where the staff would gather in off-duty moments to share stories, play games, or just enjoy one another's company. Above the fireplace was a large hooked mat embedded with a stunning formation of Canada geese flying low over the sparkling frozen snow-clad tundra. The adjacent cozy kitchenette and dining area would be the gathering place for many a spot of tea and goodies as well as our meals. True to the description in the *applicant's information* brochure, the meals were *not* varied and usually consisted of codfish in many different disguises.

When I arrived (early October 1952), the composition of the staff was in a state of flux. Several members were soon to leave on the next coastal steamer, and another nurse was due to arrive. After these changes were made, the hospital staff definitely had an international flavor—three doctors from Canada, one dentist from Scotland, one English nurse, one Canadian nurse, one Inuit nurse from the Labrador, and me from the United States. We would be "it" for the winter until the coastal steamers could navigate again in April or May and perhaps bring new recruits.

My tour of the hospital wards the next morning made me quickly appreciate the vast differences between my previous hospital milieu (Columbia-Presbyterian Medical Center in New York City) and this eighty-bed facility in nearly isolated St. Anthony, Newfoundland. (I correctly used the word "isolated" because at that time, there were no roads connecting the upper peninsula to the more populated southern part of Newfoundland or for the seventy odd miles between the northeastern and northwestern towns.) In summer, the primary means of travel was by boat. From late October to April or May, the mode was by dog team or occasional, but unpredictable, airplane. After a few days on duty, I wrote the following comments in a letter to former nursing classmates:

> Boy, I'd like to bring back from P.H. [Presbyterian Hospital] a few needed things for here, such as linen, more linen, penicillin, syringes, #22 needles (all these are #20 for I.M.'s), paper cups, paper towels, bedpan flusher, Zephiran (to replace Lysol in the forceps jars),

electrical sockets at the bedsides, floor lamps, beds that crank up, more blood pressure machines, Abbott-prepared I.V. solutions and set-ups, a blood bank, rolls of adhesive (ours come in a 12 inch wide roll that we strip into different widths and roll up on tongue depressors).

My first memorable nursing task was to administer forty streptomycin shots IM (intramuscularly) to the many tuberculosis patients. The practice consisted of filling a 10 cc. syringe, administering 1 cc. to ten patients, using a different needle and skin preparation for each, then repeating the procedure until all were completed. It seemed almost sacrilegious at the time—to be using the same syringe—but the patients experienced no untoward effects as far as we could tell.

[By 1952, the year that I arrived at the St. Anthony hospital, some strides had been made in the control of tuberculosis. I feel privileged to have been present in northern Newfoundland during those early stages that led to the eventual near eradication of tuberculosis. It had been at epidemic proportions during the 1940s (145 per 10,000 population) and the incidence in Labrador—from whence the Inuit (Eskimo) and Innu (Indian) patients came—was double that. Those with tuberculosis were not completely isolated from the other patients in the hospital and that risk was certainly not being ignored. A new fifty-five-bed sanitarium was in the process of construction and was opened the following summer. It was soon filled to capacity and remained that way until the 1960s when it was converted to staff apartments. This coincided with the opening of the much larger, well-equipped hospital that exists today.]

I soon learned that the lights and the electrical power would go off at 10:30 PM each night. The hospital buildings were on 220-volt direct current that posed many inconveniences. One way in which it affected me directly was related to the movie projector that I had brought north with me. It required 120-volt alternating current. I enlisted the help of the mission electrician who devised an arrangement to step down the current so that the projector would work. The only catch was that I had to transport two heavy pieces of electrical equipment in addition to the projector and screen when I showed cartoons such as Betty Boop or Mickey Mouse to the patients in the several wards and to the children in the orphanage; many of whom had never seen films before. They laughed and their faces glowed as they asked to see them over and over; you would think they were seeing a full-length Disney movie.

The need to carry around the heavy transformers was eliminated after a few months when the new power plant that had been in the construction stage for months was on line. The hospital staff welcomed the fact that the wards would now have electrical lighting after 10:30 at night to facilitate the evaluation and treatment of patients.

Hospital in St. Anthony 1953 (RML)

2—Piggery Barn *On Fire!*

The first of many exciting incidents occurred just days after I arrived in St. Anthony. We three nurses (the *only* three at that time) were relaxing at about 1:00 AM in the living room after a busy evening tending to patients when we heard the hospital whistle blowing off steam but without enough oomph to really sound the alarm. We dashed to the window and saw flames in the direction of the mission barn.

We grabbed our coats and boots and ran the quarter mile toward the fire, stopping on the way to awaken Dr. Thomas. Upon arrival, we found the newly constructed piggery barn fully engulfed in flames with the squealing pigs still inside their apartments. There was no way to save the barn, but, fortunately, the pigs were still accessible. We four began carrying the pigs to a safe enclosure some distance away—first the piglets by holding on to their slippery, squirming hind legs, then back and forth for more; each time the pigs were larger and heavier. Even though our clothes were a mess, we felt triumphant when every single pig was out of harm's way.

Within the hour, the barn itself had fallen down, in black shambles, except for the tall brick chimney in the center where the stove had been. Men had arrived from the radar base that was a part of the DEW line (Distant Early Warning), the system erected by the United States following World War II. The construction foreman from the base came riding in on a bulldozer, cowboy hat and all, and was raring to go. He decided that the chimney should be knocked down; after all, he had to make *some* use of his bulldozer. At one point, he got the dozer stuck amidst the rubble and broken glass and had to be pushed and pulled off by his compatriots. When that project was finished and the chimney was reduced to a pile of bricks, he noticed that his hand and wrist were bleeding profusely. Dr. Thomas quickly evaluated the injury and directed us to his Jeep. We all piled in and headed for the hospital—including our patient, Max. He was a tall, burly fellow who was born to be *in charge*.

We four went to the operating room immediately and donned the appropriate garb right over our slacks and boots. Phyllis Baird prepared the anesthesia, Pauline White was the circulating nurse, I was the scrub nurse, and of course, Dr. Thomas was the surgeon. Max had managed to cut some vital structures in his forearm requiring careful dissection and multiple sutures. We discussed the need for the wrist and forearm to remain immobile for a spell. We knew that that instruction would run counter to Max's personality and job title, so a plaster of paris cast was applied—just for good measure.

The next morning, Max wanted to get up immediately so he could get back to his job at the base and sputtered about the "damned cast." He brushed off our offers to help him get up, and as he arose, his complexion became ashen; he wavered unsteadily, and fainted. As he started his descent to the floor, we caught him and lifted him back on to his bed. Later in the day, he showed much less bravado but was able to return to the base with cast and all. During the ensuing months, he became a staunch supporter of Dr. Thomas and of the hospital and its endeavors. He repeatedly expressed his gratitude for the way in which his arm had returned so rapidly to normal in spite of—or because of— the "damned cast."

This fire was a disaster with long-term as well as the anticipated short-term consequences. The hospital and staff relied upon the mission farm for its food supplies—milk from the Holsteins, pork from the pigs, and garden produce. Other food items, such as eggs and fish, were obtained from surrounding townspeople in exchange for donated used clothing. With the long, cold winter approaching, it was essential to prepare permanent housing for those homeless pigs and piglets. This job fell to the crew that was already engaged in the construction of the new TB sanitarium, but that project had to be delayed temporarily while those men worked feverishly to construct a new piggery barn in just one month's time.

3—From Bakeapples to Babies

It was a snowy, brisk day late in November when Dr. Thomas asked if I would like to take a trip on the *Maraval* up the coast to the fishing village of Quirpon (pronounced carpoon). I was to check the status of an elderly woman with a cardiac problem and bring her back to the hospital. I jumped at the chance to go out to sea again on the *Maraval*—this time as a nurse, not just as a passenger—to see a patient in her own home and to learn more about Newfoundland customs and environs. Since my nursing duties were not yet needed, Skipper Neville asked, "Would you like to take the wheel, Miss?" I said, "Sure." And what a thrill it was to motor along the bleak, rugged coastline. Shards of ice were already forming in the bays as the rushing sea carried them in and out. Before too long the ice would "catch" and the bays would be covered over until spring.

We dropped anchor at Little Quirpon and were soon approached by a small boat being rowed by the patient's husband. I climbed down the ladder, black bag in hand, and hopped aboard for the trip to his dock. He was dressed in his oilskins and boots and had very little to say except "Yes, Miss," or "No, Miss," and "You must be right chilly, Miss." I followed him into the house expecting to find the patient in bed. Instead, there she was, being the perfect hostess with ten to twelve friends, neighbors, and relatives sitting around the perimeter of the room. She insisted that I take off my boots and warm my feet by the big black wood stove in the center. As much as my cold feet were aching, it didn't seem right to treat *them* before treating the patient, so I took her vital signs and asked a few questions. She didn't seem to mind one bit, as I did, that this was in front of all these people, but there was no place else to go. She then said, "You must join us for tea, Miss." Not only did we have tea, but also bakeapples and nut bread. (Yes, it really is bakeapples—Newfoundland's unique berries, *Rubus chamaemorus*.) To use an expression with which I was becoming very familiar, the refreshments were "some good!" (Little did I know then, or did anyone else, that Quirpon was just five and a half miles from the Viking settlement that archeologists uncovered in 1960 in L'Anse aux Meadows and has since become a National Historic Site of Canada.)

This was my introduction to a common practice in Newfoundland and Labrador for friends and relatives to gather at the home of a potential patient for the rare opportunity for each one to ask the medical visitor about one's ailments. In spite of the lack of any telephone service, it was uncanny how the people knew when someone from the hospital was going to arrive. In addition to word of mouth, some were able to listen in to the RT (radiotelephone) messages between a nurse at an outlying station and a doctor at the St. Anthony Hospital. It was always a challenge for those involved to code them in such a way as to maintain some modicum of privacy to prevent rumors, which could, and many times did, become very distorted.

With his wife bundled up for the trip, her husband led us to the dock, and we boarded the rowboat for the journey back to the *Maraval*. The winds had picked up, and the sea had become rougher in the hour and a half that we had been inside the house. It was rather risky climbing up the ladder while the rowboat banged against the side of the rocking *Maraval*. I breathed a sigh of relief when the patient and I were safely on the deck; the engine started, the anchor hauled in, and we were off. Neville said, "It's going to be rough going back, Miss. The barometer is falling."

I got the patient settled in a lower bunk in the dispensary as soon as possible. The ship was rolling mightily as we moved out of the harbour. I felt a bit queasy after putting a dressing on my finger that I had jammed under the ship's ladder. It seemed wise for me to lie down also in a nearby bunk. I checked my patient frequently as the ship rolled and pitched, presuming she must be feeling as ill as I was, but each time, she said, "I feels fine, Miss."

When we finally reached the safe, landlocked harbour of St. Anthony, I could see in the distance that the coastal steamer, *Springdale*, was in the process of tying up to the mission wharf. This was odd because she wasn't expected for another day or two. As our ship approached the dock, we saw Dr. Thomas waving at us impatiently, and his first words were, "Grab the equipment from the *Maraval* and meet me on the *Springdale*. We've got a delivery to do on board." One of the aides, Lizzie, was also there, ready to take my elderly patient up to the hospital in a Jeep. I quickly said to her, "Good-bye. See you later at the hospital."

4—Delivery Onboard the SS *Springdale*

After Dr. Thomas said "meet me on the *Springdale*. We've got a delivery to do on board," I quickly gathered everything that I thought we would need and ran to the ship now tied up to the wharf. I found Dr. Thomas and the new patient in the ship's lounge. The patient was obviously very far along in labor, contractions every two minutes or less, so there was no time to get her to the hospital. (The *Springdale* had skipped several ports of call in order to get the woman to St. Anthony in time for delivery. It made it just in time!)

SS Springdale, *Coastal Steamer*
(*Courtesy of Railway Coastal Museum, St. John's*)

We quickly cleared the ship's lounge of curious onlookers, pulled the window drapes, placed the patient on a wall bench, and pulled up a table for the improvised equipment. There was barely time to do the usual preparation, and as I was checking the fetal heart rate, the baby's head appeared. I called to Dr. Thomas, who was assembling additional equipment nearby, "You'd better come over here, *stat!*" After a few minutes, it was apparent that this baby did not want to budge, and Dr. Thomas said, "I've got to do an episiotomy. Give her a little ether." While he made the incision, I administered open-drop ether. Soon the eight-pound ten-ounce baby girl was out and put forth a welcomed lusty cry. After tying the cord, Dr. Thomas handed the baby to Lizzie, the aide who had just returned. She bundled the baby into a blanket, wrapped her in an army jacket that she had been wearing, and whisked her off to the hospital in a workman's truck.

In the next half hour, Dr. Thomas sutured the episiotomy, administered some pituitrin, and completed the postpartum care. When the patient was stable enough, he drove her up to the hospital in the Jeep. Meanwhile, I had the responsibility of restoring the lounge to its former condition. That process was relatively simple because I would take almost everything back to the hospital: linens, rubber gloves, syringes, needles, IV sets, scissors, and scalpels. There, they would be washed, sterilized, and reused many more times. I gathered up everything into two bundles, but—alas!—there was one item left. The disposal of which had me baffled — *the placenta!* I was too shy to ask any crewmember for an appropriate place, and I couldn't just put it in one of the wastebaskets. I came up with a great idea: I carried it in a basin to the opposite side of the ship where there was nary a soul and quietly tossed it overboard. I was confident that it would sink to the very bottom, never to be seen again. Much to my shock, there it was, floating on the surface, bobbing along merrily next to the ship's hull. I couldn't retrieve it, so I left it, hoping that no one on board would spot it and that someday, if a future mariner should find it, he might think he had discovered a new species of aquatic life.

The mother stayed in the hospital until she was ready for discharge. As she boarded the next steamer headed in her home direction, she held in her arms a beautiful, healthy, rosy-cheeked, little girl whom she had named *Dale* as a reminder of her unusual birthplace—aboard the coastal steamer, *Springdale*.

5—Sports Day: Dog Team Race

One tradition that was eagerly anticipated both by the townspeople and the mission staff was Sports Day. It always seemed to perk up spirits during that long winter period when the harbour ice was frozen solid and all navigation was nonexistent.

The dog team races were popular events: one for the men, and one for the women. It sounded like great fun to me, and I felt confident that I could do it. Despite never having driven a team, I signed up for the race and made arrangements to borrow a team from a local dog team owner/driver, Kie Patey, and it wasn't just any old team. It had just won the men's race—a fact which further bolstered my confidence.

"Komatik" is the Inuit word for sled. Ours was eight to nine feet long with long runners curved upward in the front for about three feet. This feature allowed the komatik to turn sharply, if necessary, in the deep snow and wooded areas. It also made it possible for the driver to be at the front end of the sled, at times, and use the runners as handles when maneuvering over tough terrain. The komatik cousin, used in Alaska and the Arctic, had lower and more sharply curved runners that were adequate for those wide open spaces, often on the ice.

We brought our teams to the foot of the mission wharf to listen to the rules and instructions for the once-around-the-harbour course. I glanced to my left and then to my right and realized there were only three other teams. *This should be easy,* I said to myself. *After all, I have the fastest team of dogs, and haven't I had a few sports achievements of my own?*

We jockeyed our teams into position on the starting line. I hopped on the rear of the komatik just as the starter said "Ready, set, *go!*" with the simultaneous crack of the pistol. We took off like a rocket before I even had a chance to give the dogs *my* signal to go. I barely managed to stay on board. Soon the team settled down to a nice smooth pace for the next quarter of a mile, and we were in the lead by several lengths. Just as my confidence returned, we reached the bottom of the harbour, and the course took a turn to the right, but my team followed their intrepid lead dog and veered off to the left. I shouted "k'poff, k'poff" (keep off) as I had heard the men do when they wanted to turn right. The opposite command was "hody, hody, hody" (hold in) to go left. Nothing I did or said dissuaded them as we bounced over the terrain and between fences toward their destination. Those fine dogs must have sensed that they had a novice on board *their* komatik. Finally they stopped abruptly at the rear of a house with a large fenced-in area for dogs. It was their very own kennel and home!

The team's owner/driver, Kie, back at the starting line could see my plight and came to my rescue as soon as he could. He untangled the dogs and traces, turned the komatik around in the right direction, and with a crack of his whip, sent us flying off back on course again. I could just see the other three teams way off in the distance. Although my team was making very good time (and staying on the course) we crossed the finish line *dead last!*

6—Operating Room Nurse—*and More*

From 1952 to 1954 I was in charge of the operating room at St. Anthony. I had never had any OR experience as a graduate, but my student elective stint at Columbia-Presbyterian Hospital in New York was rigorous enough to embolden me to consent to this challenge.

Dr. Gordon Thomas performed a great variety of surgical procedures—everything from tonsillectomies to neurosurgery—and many of them were done because of tuberculosis. At that period of time, its incidence in northern Newfoundland and Labrador was of epidemic proportions and the highest in North America. For the treatment of this disease, the use of the drug streptomycin was in its infancy, which left surgery as the principal means of treatment, at least in the far north. Procedures included pneumothorax (collapse of the lung by injection of air), thoracoplasty (collapse of lung in stages by removal of ribs), lobectomy (removal of a diseased segment of the lung), and pneumonectomy (removal of the right or left lung).

[It is interesting and rewarding to note that twenty years later, Dr. Gordon W. Thomas reported, "By 1972 the disease was so nearly under control and drug treatment so effective that we performed no more elective surgery for pulmonary tuberculosis." There were many contributing factors to this rosy outcome—drug therapy was an obvious one, equally important were the improvement in the peoples' nutritional status, and the earlier detection of the tubercle bacillus. The latter was greatly enhanced by the more modern means of transportation and communication that allowed the patients to be located and evaluated earlier. The Canadian government's increasing financial responsibility for the remote areas of the province played a big part in this. The role that the Grenfell Mission played in the near eradication of tuberculosis was indeed one of its most outstanding achievements during its long history since being founded by Sir Wilfred Grenfell in the 1890s.]

In this new environment, I quickly learned that, in addition to being a scrub nurse during an operation, there were many other preparatory responsibilities—chief of which was to produce sterile supplies: instruments, intravenous solutions, linens (surgical drapes, doctor's gowns), and rubber gloves for the entire hospital.

None of the equipment was disposable, with the resulting requirement that the instruments had to be oiled and/or sharpened as needed, and that the linens be washed (by the laundry). The gloves had to be washed and tested for leaks by blowing into them, and then they had to be powdered and packaged. All these items were sterilized in the OR, and specific surgical sets were assembled for each type of surgical procedure. As the OR nurse, I prepared all of the intravenous therapy sets for the entire hospital as well as mixed and prepared the solutions (normal saline, dextrose and saline, dextrose and water, etc.). There were no commercially prepared IV sets or premixed solutions, so the procedure was to place the newly prepared solution in a one thousand-cubic centimeter flask, plug the neck with gauze, cover the top with a square of brown paper, and secure it with a piece of string (this allowed for expansion while in the autoclave). When a specific solution was ordered for a patient, its flask was emptied into a calibrated sterile glass container with rubber tubing attached to an outflow stem at the bottom. The sterilization of all these items fell on the shoulders of one ancient steam autoclave. While listening to its constant hissing and spitting, I often thought it was about to explode. It had to be watched and treated carefully and could never be left alone.

The latest and best equipment for surgery was not always available, and on several occasions, Dr. Thomas enlisted the expertise of men from the machine shop to devise a necessary piece. Just a few years earlier, there was no electric cautery in the OR, so the self-taught hospital electrician and Dr. Thomas devised one from an old deep-heat, short-wave machine that had been designed for physiotherapy. They also jury-rigged, out of a heavy-duty can opener from the hospital kitchen, an instrument to spread the ribs apart for the first chest operations that were performed at St. Anthony in the late 1940s.

There were many nonsterile items for the entire hospital that had to be prepared. Adhesive tape that was stuck to crinoline arrived in twelve-inch-wide rolls. In order to make the tape manageable, we (nurses, aides, and, at times, patients) would tear the different widths (one-half inch, one inch, and two inches) from the roll and wind those strips onto wooden tongue depressors. Some of the discarded crinoline would be used later to make Vaseline gauze strips for the treatment of certain wounds.

Body casts were used for many patients with tuberculosis of the spine who required immobilization. These necessitated the use of many rolls of plaster of paris. The OR nurse was responsible for making these by cutting a large roll of crinoline into the proper widths, dragging each piece through a large metal tray filled with the powdered plaster, and then rolling them. To make the body cast, the patient (usually a child) was placed in a body-size stockinette from head to toe and then wrapped tediously with multiple rolls of wet plaster until he or she looked like an Egyptian mummy —and *probably felt like one.* The patient lay on the table, unable to move until the cast was dry. Meanwhile, the cast was getting uncomfortably warm due to the chemical reaction between the plaster and water. After a period, that must have seemed endless to the patient, the cast was opened with an electric saw, its blade guided very carefully along both sides as the patient watched with great trepidation until at last he, or she, could breathe a sigh of relief. The edges of the cast were properly trimmed, padded, and the end result resembled a divided clamshell. The patient then could lie on either the top or the bottom half for several hours until the nurse strapped on the opposite piece of the shell, turned the patient, and then removed the other piece. This procedure could go on for many long months. I cannot say enough about the patience and stamina of those who went through this uncomfortable ordeal. I saw another example of the easy-going, solid, good nature of the Newfoundlanders and Inuits (Eskimos).

I had to maintain an adequate supply of gas tanks—primarily of oxygen and nitrous oxide. When more were required, we sent Johnny Mitchell, the handyman, down to the mission store for one or more. It seemed a strange and inconvenient place to store them, and I can only assume they were kept there because of lack of space at the hospital, and/or for safety reasons.

The mention of oxygen reminds me of a morning when I was attaching a valve to a large tank of oxygen prior to surgery. The wrench slipped off the nut and into my face just below my lower lip cutting through into my mouth. Fortunately my teeth remained intact. Before we could start the planned surgical procedure, Dr. Gordon Gray injected some Novocain into my chin and put in a few sutures. The injection hurt more than anything else. Then we proceeded as scheduled with the main surgery of the morning.

Some surgical procedures we knew in advance would require a blood transfusion. In the absence of a blood bank, a donor list was maintained of townspeople and staff with blood types and addresses. The required donor would come in the day before the scheduled surgery and give the blood that was then refrigerated. On occasion, in the middle of an operation, it was necessary to find an immediate donor. Johnny Mitchell, as usual, was sent to bring that donor back to the hospital. (With no telephone communication and few roads, Johnny would often go on foot for this errand.) During one emergency operation, as blood spurted from a nicked artery, it was apparent that blood would be needed immediately. The donor list contained no one with the patient's Rh-negative blood type, except for the OR nurse (me); so on the spot, I became the donor and within a few minutes returned to the scrub nurse role.

There were many times when a physician was not available to assist Dr. Thomas in surgery. The second doctor might be involved with some emergency, a delivery, or perhaps away on a medical tour up the coast during a flu epidemic, or for some other purpose. On those occasions, I would become the first assistant with another nurse (or an aide) acting as the scrub nurse. Those were exciting times as I learned how to hold the retractors correctly, suction, tie off blood vessels, etc.

With the prevalence of tuberculosis in the hospital, it was a challenge to keep the operating room in an aseptic condition. I was always mindful that it also functioned as a delivery suite for difficult births. I must give credit to my surgical instructors at Columbia-Presbyterian Hospital for the rigid and well-practiced training that I had received in sterile technique. I cannot recall any case of infection to which the source was attributed to the OR while I was at St. Anthony.

The OR schedule was very irregular, depending upon the time of year, the arrival of the coastal steamer with her many potential surgical patients, the availability of the surgeon (because he also was called away on medical trips and/or emergencies), and the occasional arrival of surgical specialists who volunteered their services (particularly in the summer).

Some of my readers may be interested in a more detailed account of the variety of surgical procedures and will understand the medical terminology. Since this is not intended to be an instructional story, I will not attempt to define each one.

I was pleasantly surprised to find, among my records from 1952, an actual listing of nineteen surgical days. Of the forty-one procedures that were completed, there were the following:

Three incisions and drainages of wounds
Three biopsies
Three D & Cs
One mid-thigh leg amputation
One resection of hyoid bone and radium implant
One cystoscopy
Three herniorrhaphies

One closed reduction of fibula with cast application
One exploratory laparotomy
One lobectomy (middle lobe)
Three cyst removals (eye, hand, cervix)
One embolectomy
One hydrocele reduction
One caesarian section
One paraffin pack (with subsequent cardiac massage)
One radium implant in mouth
One reduction of Colles' fracture with cast application
Two third-stage thoracoplasties
Two bronchoscopies
One dermatome graft to ankle
One phrenic nerve crush
Two cast renewals
One open reduction and plating of femur
One cholecystectomy
One club foot procedure
One frontal craniotomy
One appendectomy
One hemorrhoidectomy

In a normal hospital setting, these procedures would usually be performed by surgeons from the following specialties: general surgery, orthopedics, plastic surgery, otolaryngology, obstetrics-gynecology, neurosurgery, oncologic surgery, urology, and ophthalmological surgery.

[I still marvel that all these operations—and many more procedures not even included here—were done solely by Dr. Gordon Thomas with the assistance of doctors who had had very little training in surgery. He was truly an outstanding surgeon as well as medical doctor and was with the Grenfell Mission for thirty-three years, overseeing its evolution from private charity to government-sponsored service.

Although he was only thirty-two years old when I worked with him in St. Anthony, his achievements are more easily understood when realizing the outstanding medical educational background that he had. For example, he interned at the Montreal Neurological Institute under the world-famous Canadian neurosurgeon, Dr. Wilder Penfield. In fact, it was through Dr. Penfield's efforts that Dr. Thomas was able to acquire the original shipment of streptomycin in the late 1940s. After retirement, Dr. Thomas wrote a fascinating account of his tenure at St. Anthony—*From Sled to Satellite: My Years with the Grenfell Mission.*]

Dr. Gordon Thomas and Rosalie Lombard (RML)

Ivy Durley (RML)

7—Dog Team Trip to Flower's Cove

It was in February of 1953 that Dr. Thomas posed the question "How would you like to go on a dog team trip?" "*Yes!* I'd love to," I said without hesitation, even before hearing the details. I would be going to the Flower's Cove nursing station to replace Ivy Durley, the English nurse-midwife, for a two-week period. She was expected to arrive in St Anthony the very next day and take my place at the hospital. After several months of being isolated from the outside world, it sounded like it would be a beneficial change for each of us and would also give us experience in a different aspect of medical care within the Grenfell Mission—a still commonly used term in 1953 even though it was technically obsolescent.

Dog team travel at that time of year was the only way to get to Flower's Cove, almost seventy miles west of St. Anthony. Tom Macey, dog team driver from Green Island Brook, would be bringing Ivy to the hospital and then returning with his new passenger (me). Tom was widely known and respected for his reliability, resourcefulness, and superb treatment of his high-quality team of dogs.

With little time to spare, I prepared for the trip by gathering plenty of layers of warm underclothing, seal skin boots, socks, mittens, ski cap, goggles, parka, overalls, snow shoes, movie camera, sleeping bag, and toiletries.

The morning after Ivy's arrival, we were almost ready to depart. Outside, near the hospital's front door, I watched with interest as Tom packed the komatik, skillfully "threw out the traces" for each of the eight dogs, harnessed them, and announced that we were ready to go. With a crack of his whip, the barking dogs were off and away with great haste but soon slowed down for the trek up Fox Farm Hill just to the rear of the hospital. Tom and I walked behind the komatik to lighten the load for the dogs. At the top, we passed by the grave of Dr. Wilfred Grenfell, although it was not visible under the many feet of snow.

We headed west over the frozen ponds, through woods, and up and down the hills. At times I rode in the coach box with Tom standing on the rear of the komatik. When the trail was narrow or steep, he stayed at the front of the sled, partially suspended in air, holding on precariously to the long curved ends of the runners, jamming his feet down occasionally to help turn the sled, or to brake the speed and keep the komatik from running into the dogs. At times the going was rough, and when we needed to lighten the load for the dogs, I would walk or run along behind the sled—with snowshoes or sometimes without. Once in a while, during the long stretches, it became necessary to tell Tom to "Go on ahead, and I'll catch up to you in a minute." He knew exactly what I meant. He had transported many a Grenfell nurse before me. I suspect that he also made good use of that time—although with much less struggle than I.

We traveled all day, with the temperature steadily dropping, until the sun—in all its glory—was ready to set. It seemed as if that particular sunset had all the colors of the rainbow reflecting on the pure glistening snow and was created especially for this one particular adventure of mine. My prized movie camera turned out to be not so prized. Many times when I tried to catch an unforgettable moment, it would not work. I found that the mechanism would freeze in the below-freezing temperatures. I learned to keep it warm under many layers next to my body. That would work for a short span, but it was very uncomfortable putting the cold camera back inside my clothing.

In the distance, we saw smoke curling from the chimney of a small log cabin. These tilts were built by the dog team drivers and spaced at strategic intervals along the trails. As we approached the tilt, we could see three komatiks and many dogs burrowed into the snow. We were soon greeted heartily by their six drivers, all of whom knew Tom and one another. Tom's very first job was to feed his hungry dogs after their strenuous day up and down the trail.

We unloaded our gear into the tilt where I saw the eight wooden bunks attached to the walls. At one end of the room was the black woodstove already fired up, making the inside temperature much cozier than the below zero outside. Nearby sat the large empty tin cans that would be the cooking pots. The only bunks available, understandably, were furthermost from the stove. As I started to claim one of those, a big husky fellow stopped me and insisted that I take his—the choicest one next to the fire. I readily accepted the offer.

Tom Macey and the tilt on the trail to Flower's Cove (RML)

Rosalie Lombard in winter garb (RML)

Tom Macey and Seal (RML)

So here we were—seven men and one woman—about to spend the night in a tilt. It would seem natural to assume that this might create some problems or at the least some awkwardness— but not so. These men seemed to hold the Grenfell nurses and doctors in high esteem. They would never act in a way that would betray that trust.

Tom produced some vittles from the "grub box," melted snow for tea water, and we sat around the stove for a meal, which, though sparse, tasted like it came directly from heaven. As delightful as that was, the highlight for me was listening to the harrowing tales of dog team adventures that these men had experienced. The stories went on and on, and I hated to leave, but it became necessary to excuse myself and return to the frigid cold outside for an urgent calling. The night was peaceful and beautiful with a wonderful display of northern lights—streaks of color bouncing off the snow. All twenty to thirty dogs were snug in their burrows. While admiring the beauty, I was reminded of my primary goal. The task was not easy, however. First came the lowering of the five layers of obstruction—overalls, ski pants, wool slacks, snuggies, and panties. Then, just at the crucial moment, the dogs awakened and all hell broke loose. They barked and howled like a canine glee club, and it was a challenge to fend off the cold noses of this curious band of intruders.

Back inside, the stories and mugs of hot tea continued until one by one the men took to their bunks. During the night, periodically, I could hear someone getting up to put more wood in the stove. Snug as I was in my down sleeping bag, I thought, *Am I glad that it is not my responsibility.*

I awoke around seven in the morning to the sound of barking and found the men already outside the tilt harnessing their dogs, who seemed eager to get started on the new day's journey. Just then along came another driver with a small team pulling a komatik upon which a large dead seal was tethered. The man already had made his catch for the day and was headed home. He stopped long enough to share breakfast with Tom and me. We had bread, toasted on top of the woodstove and tea before we headed in opposite directions toward our next stops.

This day went by rapidly. Because of the relatively flat terrain, I was able to stay in the coach box with only an occasional need to snowshoe behind the komatik. As the shadows lengthened and the temperature dropped to near zero, we began to see a few houses as we neared Green Island Brook. This was Tom's home, and the plan was to stay there overnight. As soon as we arrived, his wife quickly prepared a meal, even though she could not have known the hour, or even the day, that we would arrive. In the center of the room was the black woodstove that was the sole source of heat for the house. After the meal, there were many relatives and neighbors gathered around the perimeter of the room, listening intently to Tom's account of his absence. Of special interest was his sojourn in St. Anthony as most of them had never been there and were eager for to hear all about it and his trip.

Eventually, I was shown to my bed in the only room on the second floor. I did not know whom I was displacing, only that I had been given the choicest bed in the house. Even though the temperature in the room during the night must have been in the forties or fifties, I was snug under many layers of blankets, so heavy that I could barely move.

I was awakened in the morning by the wonderful aroma of coffee—not tea! What a welcome treat along with the toast and jam. Soon we were again on our way to complete the last leg of our trip from St. Anthony to Flower's Cove. Only a short distance remained—ten miles or so. I anxiously awaited the experiences that were ahead, filling in for a very capable and revered nurse-midwife, in this remote area of northern Newfoundland. As the nursing station came into view, I wondered what the days ahead would hold and whether I would be up to the task.

8—Flu Epidemic in the North

Upon arrival at Flower's Cove Nursing Station, I was greeted by Win Burgess, the English nurse-midwife. After saying "good-bye" to Tom and his dogs, Win and I unloaded my bags in a bedroom upstairs. Then the first order of business was to sit down for a "spot of tea" while she oriented me to the general geographic area and what our duties would entail. This was followed by a tour of the facilities and equipment and their use.

I was awakened quietly, early the next morning by an aide bearing a tray containing tea and toast. Putting milk in tea was a new custom for me, but according to my new English friend, it was the only way to go. This was a royal welcome to my home for the next two weeks; I was not accustomed to having breakfast in bed.

Meanwhile, downstairs in the waiting room, there was quite a different picture. Already at 7:00 AM, there were three mothers assembled with their fussy, sick babies who were crying, spitting up, with noses running at full tilt. One child was badly dehydrated and needed fluids. After trying unsuccessfully to administer them orally, then intravenously, the only method left was by clysis. This had never been included in my training at Presbyterian, but I accomplished it under the supervision of Win while she cared for the several other patients.

This was the onset of a serious flu epidemic, which would last for the remainder of my visit. Both nurse Win and I were to have many nights with few, or no, hours of sleep. Daily, she would call on the RT (radiotelephone) at the noon "sched" with Dr. Thomas in St. Anthony to obtain his advice for the best forms of treatment.

One small child, who was already critical, did die at the nursing station. We wondered if her body or certain organs could be sent to St. Anthony, whether a clue could be found as to the exact organism involved, so that others would benefit from the appropriate treatment.

After discussion with Dr. Thomas on the RT, this plan was deemed not practical, nor judicious, for many reasons—least of which was the sixty-mile trip by dog team that would be required.

The Flower's Cove station covered the St. Barbe coast from Castor River to Eddie's Cove, a district seventy miles long containing over two thousand people. There was another nursing station, Forteau, only seven miles away, but the two were separated by the Gulf of St. Lawrence in the section known as the Straits of Belle Isle. The only contact these nurses had with one another during the long winter months was by chatting on the RT. Only in a rare winter, when the gulf was totally iced over, could they visit in person or share resources. Their rigorous schedules usually precluded even that.

The two-week period passed quickly with a continual influx of sick, very dehydrated babies. There were also a few adults with the flu, but mostly they were at the nursing station for a variety of other ailments, and Win delivered several babies by normal delivery.

At the end of my visit, Win told me that I had gotten a snapshot of a typical two-week *winter* period, that the summer presents a variety of different problems related to the fishing industry (e.g., injuries from fishhooks, cuts and bruises, fractures, etc.).

The flu epidemic was also occurring in many other places on the Labrador. After my return to St. Anthony, there were many RT calls asking for help as far up the coast as Nain. A plane was engaged to take Dr. Gordon Gray to many of the settlements with a supply of medications to be administered. Pauline White, a nurse of Inuit descent, went along to translate and to assist him.

Ted McNeill, Dr. Gordon Gray, and his wife, Mary Gray (RML)

It was always necessary and judicious to make the best use of the rare airplane flight, so there were other passengers—three Inuit men to return to their Labrador homes after several months of treatment at the hospital. Two of them had tuberculosis surgery and the third was treated for severe hypothermia and related problems. He and his team of dogs had been trapped on an ice floe for days after it had broken away from the mainland ice.

The last passenger was Dr. Tom Kennedy, a dentist from Scotland. Two of us pulled a sled precariously loaded with his equipment, including a dental drill operated by foot pedals. The whole load tipped over during the trek.

Marilyn Tolley loading the foot-pedaled dental drill (RML)

Inuits returning to Labrador (RML)

The airstrip on the harbour ice was covered with several feet of snow. The runway was prepared by using a giant snow blower, probably operated by the corps of engineers from the radar base.

Many of the staff members from the hospital were involved in transporting patients and equipment to the plane and saying their last minute good-byes to these Inuits who had been at the hospital for many weeks and had become more than just patients. We all waved as the plane zoomed down the runway and off to Labrador, barely rising above the bluff at the bottom of the harbour.

Rosalie Lombard saying good-bye to a patient from Labrador (RML)

9—Potpourri of Embarrassing Moments

My First Night On Call

During my first winter in St. Anthony, in addition to our daytime duties, we nurses were on call every third night. The nurses' aides covered the evening and night shifts, but the nurse would be called— to give certain medications, to admit a new patient, for a delivery or operation, or for any emergency.

On my very *first* night on call, an aide came knocking on my door at 2:00 AM to announce a woman in labor had just appeared. I quickly dressed appropriately and arrived on the ward to find a seventeen-year-old girl and her husband. She told me that she was seven months along and was having "scattered pains."

My obstetrical training as a student had been minimal, but I knew in general the kinds of questions to ask and the composition of the initial exam. I did both to the best of my ability but not with my usual confidence. During the half hour while she was in my presence, I could barely detect her reacting to her contractions like so many of my patients in New York City had done.

I had to decide if this was a situation for which I should send a messenger to awaken Dr. Erb who was on call (whom I knew had already been working late and didn't live in the hospital building as we nurses did). I knew I would be embarrassed if I called him and it turned out to be completely unnecessary.

I reviewed mentally the results of my examination and the information gleaned from the patient: she was only seven months pregnant, contractions did not seem to cause much discomfort, and my exam did not reveal any signs of imminent labor. I had learned about Braxton-Hicks contractions associated with false labor during my limited obstetrical training at Columbia-Presbyterian. I came to the conclusion that this seven-month pregnant young girl was so anxious about her first baby that she had convinced herself and/or her husband that she was in labor. I attempted to reassure them and explained that she was probably feeling false labor pains, that she should return home and get a good night's sleep (what there was left of it). I told her if the pains continued, she should come into the hospital the next day. I went back to my room at 3:00 AM, pleased that it hadn't been necessary to send for the doctor and proud that I had remembered about those Braxton-Hicks contractions. I fell fast asleep.

At 6:00 AM, an aide came knocking on my door again with the news that the same patient was back. After taking a quick look at her this time, there were obvious signs of labor, plus her contractions were every two minutes or less and were difficult to miss. I sent one of the aides to get Dr. Erb immediately, and I prepped the patient for delivery. It wasn't too long before she delivered an eight-pound baby. When Dr. Erb asked why she had not come in earlier, I had to explain, with a very red face, that, actually she *had* come in earlier but *I* sent her home.

This episode didn't quite fit the picture for a seven-month pregnancy, and I learned the reason later. The truth was that this young patient was *nine* months pregnant but hadn't been married that long, so the seven-month story probably had helped to make the couple feel a little better about their situation. Also, I learned that in Newfoundland, women in labor were much more laid back and calm compared to my patients back in New York City. (I remember one patient at St. Anthony who was in labor with her third child. All during the final stages of labor, she was telling us an interesting story. With each contraction, she paused but then continued the story right where she had left off. In fact, even after the baby appeared on the scene, she continued until her story was finished).

Thanksgiving Day, November 20, 1952 — or is it?

In November of 1952, there was a nice variety of staff members from England, Canada, Scotland, Newfoundland and Labrador, and three of us from the United States.

The Canadian Thanksgiving had been celebrated as usual in October, and we three, Marilyn Tolley, Van (Agnes Van Nostrand),

and I, decided we should have a special American Thanksgiving all by ourselves. Chickens were raised at the orphanage primarily for the eggs, but Van, who was in charge of the orphanage, determined that we were eligible to have a chicken for dinner since a traditional turkey was nowhere to be found. (Chicken was really special because we had had none since arriving in St. Anthony.) We each were responsible for a particular part of the meal and rounded up our items from various places—the hospital kitchen, the grocery store, and the mission barn. Van even found a can of cranberry sauce in the orphanage larder.

On November 20, 1952, after the children had had their meal, we decorated the dining room in the orphanage with handmade turkey drawings, pictures of pumpkins, donned the pilgrim paper hats that we had made, and sat down to a festive occasion. We really felt so good knowing that we were celebrating Thanksgiving at the same time as our friends and families at home.

We gathered that evening in the living room of the hospital and were smugly announcing the special Thanksgiving that we had shared when one of the staff members interrupted and said she had just heard something on the radio that they were busy in New York preparing for *next Thursday*'s Macy's Thanksgiving parade. We had had our big celebration *a week early*. We were the butt of their jokes about the crazy Americans who don't even know when their Thanksgiving is.

We felt a little better when we learned later that US President Harry Truman had meddled with the customary date (the third Thursday in November) and declared Thanksgiving to be one week later, November 27, 1952.

Which Way to St. Anthony?

This story was told to me as actual fact by an experienced dog team driver in that tilt on the trail to Flower's Cove. The other five men swore to it, as did my driver, Tom Macey.

The previous winter friends of his were on their way to St. Anthony with their teams of dogs when a terrible blizzard suddenly appeared.

The snow was blinding, and the visibility could be measured in yards. Suddenly they heard a strange whirring noise that sounded like a huge bee. Out of the mist and landing right beside them was a *helicopter!* The dogs were spooked and barked so loudly that the pilot had to shut down his engine as he poked his head out of the cabin and said, "*I'm lost.* Can you tell me which way to St. Anthony?" The dog team driver said to him, "You see that hill over there? You go up to the top and wait for me. When I get there I'll point out the way for ye." The helicopter pilot could barely see the hill, but followed those instructions implicitly and was able to safely arrive at St. Anthony only after the driver pointed him in the right direction from the top of that hill.

To the dog team drivers of Newfoundland, this was certain proof of the superiority and necessity of dog power versus air power in that part of the world, and you can be sure that that story was repeated again and again.

[As incredulous as this story may sound, the reader should bear in mind that in the early 1950s, there was no airport in St. Anthony nor was there a VOR (VHF omnidirectional range) system for air navigation. In fact, it wasn't until 1976 that this system was introduced to the St. John's airport.]

Dr. Charles Curtis and Rosalie Lombard (RML)

Dr. Charles Curtis, Pauline White, Phyllis Baird, Margaret Seaman (RML)

Part IV

The Greatest Adventure of All: Voyage on the Northern Messenger

Preface: How It All Started

In the spring of 1953, in St. Anthony, Newfoundland, as the days grew warmer and longer, you could hear the groaning and crackling of the ice as it struggled to prepare for the shipping traffic that soon would pile up, waiting to get into the landlocked harbour. If you had looked out beyond the shore fifty yards or so, you would have seen a sunken vessel with its two masts aslant above the ice that shackled her for the long winter. In April of 1953, the once proud ship, the *Northern Messenger*, built in 1917, was now rendered helpless. In her bygone days, she had sailed proudly, up and down the coasts of Newfoundland and Labrador, carrying many patients to and from the St. Anthony hospital, her canvas sails filled with that nippy Newfoundland air. One could just imagine how she must now be murmuring, *"Unleash me, and let me sail these seas again."* Many of the observers who saw her predicament over that long, hard winter predicted that the ship was doomed and that she would never sail again, but the real sailors and ship workers knew that she was a sound, seaworthy vessel. We chose to put our faith in them.

The sunken Northern Messenger, *two months before the voyage (RML)*

In her glory days, the *Northern Messenger* was a fine forty-foot, ketch-rigged, thirteen-ton ship, stabilized, when under sail, by her seven-ton keel. When becalmed or while navigating those tricky coves and tickles (narrow passageways) along the coast of Labrador and Newfoundland, her twenty-five horsepower Gray Marine inboard engine was used. We were told that Sir Wilfred Grenfell himself was at the helm on many an occasion.

Charles Currie, who graduated from MIT with a degree in naval architecture and marine engineering, had supervised the construction of the newly opened power plant that supplied the hospital buildings. He saw the potential in that forlorn hulk trapped in the ice and determined to bring her back to life despite numerous admonitions from the naysayers. He was able to negotiate the purchase of the ship for a pittance, arranged to have her righted, and hauled into the dry dock on June 20, 1953. The men labored on her for days—caulking the hull with oakum (pronounced "hokum" in Newfoundland), restoring the engine, repairing many damaged parts of the structure, and finally painting her wooden hull a vivid nile green. (I was amazed to learn, sixty-one years later, that the total charge for all that work was $212.48.)

Northern Messenger *in dry dock, one month before the voyage (RML)*

Charlie's goal was to sail her down to Boston Harbor near his home in Massachusetts, where he hoped to enjoy many sailing trips with his family and friends. However, he realized he couldn't make that voyage alone. He needed a crew of four or five to sail her across the northern tip of Newfoundland, down through the Straits of Belle Isle, and into the Gulf of St. Lawrence. At Port aux Basques, the projected route would cross over to Cape North on Cape Breton Island and into the Atlantic, through the Bay of Fundy and down the coast of Maine to Boston Harbor. Charlie calculated that with a little luck the voyage could be done in about five to ten days, in plenty of time for him to be there for the birth of his first child. (We later realized that the key phrase was *"with a little luck."*)

Charlie found four adventuresome souls who enthusiastically volunteered their services even though their sailing experience was either modest or nil.

John Jenkins, a Canadian whose work assignment was over after the completed construction of the radar base in St. Anthony (an important station of the early warning system, established up and down the North American east coast following World War II), was already enrolled in the medical school of Dalhousie University in Halifax and scheduled to begin studies in August.

Marilyn Tolley, an American recent graduate of Vassar College who worked in the orphanage as an assistant and had completed her year's commitment before returning to her home in the states.

Peggy Armstrong, a Canadian artist who had been working with the Grenfell industrial department was also due to leave for Toronto. Although professing no previous sailing experience she said, "I think it would be fun to go on a yachting trip."

Rosalie Lombard, who was scheduled for a four-week break and intended to visit relatives in the Boston area before returning to her duties as the operating room nurse in St. Anthony.

In June of 1953, the *Northern Messenger* was out of dry dock at last, launched via the marine railway back into the familiar briny, though now iceless, sea. She was moored at one of the small piers where one could easily see that her resurrection was not fully accomplished. Much more scraping, painting, outfitting, and stocking of supplies had to be done. The fearless crewmembers spent every available moment when off-duty preparing her for the journey during June and July. Most of the hours had to be during the evenings. One of John's assignments was to scrape and paint the main mast while hauled up by the halyard in a sling. Meanwhile, Marilyn and I did the same to the wheelhouse and hatch area. Charlie was responsible for bringing the outmoded engine back to life and after much tinkering and frustration finally announced success. Peggy worked on the interior, making a curtain to divide the head from the cabin, outfitting the six bunks—three upper and three lower—and finding a few used pots and kitchen utensils. On many evenings, we had curious visitors who were usually free with their ominous predictions for our voyage. We confidently tried to ignore them and continued with our preparations. Sometimes they were duly impressed when we tossed a fish line over the side, bringing up a good-sized codfish. (No need, really, to specify "cod" because in those days, fish only referred to cod.) They watched as we cleaned and fried the twenty-inch prize on our antique cast-iron woodstove. We were proud to demonstrate our newly refurbished stove from which we had scraped layer after layer of rust acquired over the winter as it lay at the bottom of the salty sea.

John Jenkins painting the mast of the Northern Messenger *(RML)*

Marilyn Tolley cleaning codfish on board Northern Messenger *(RML)*

*Rosalie Lombard and Marilyn Tolley working
on the* Northern Messenger *(RML)*

As the days drew nearer to our departure date, we three women were responsible for getting the necessary food and cleaning supplies for the first week. We had lots of storage space under the lower bunks and in racks mounted along the walls. Charlie and John had the more difficult task of collecting life preservers, boat hook, bilge pump, flashlights, small dinghy and oars, gasoline, lines, anchors, and navigational equipment (i.e., compass, barometer, charts, parallel rule, and dividers). It would have been easy to go to a marine supply store for these things, but there was no such facility there or on most of our Newfoundland/Labrador route. Similarly, there was no store from which you could purchase spare parts for our ancient engine. Charlie and John had to comb the local area for clues as to who might have extras of these items. Ultimately, they did find most of the necessary items, but many were by no means ideal. (e.g., the latest navigational chart found for the Gulf of St. Lawrence was from 1895, as I recall.)

We crew members were now living on board ship, and in our eyes, the *Northern Messenger* looked pretty spiffy and journey ready (except for some painting, which we could easily complete while sailing). We were getting restless and ached to get started on this new adventure. The last essential was accomplished when the immigration officer boarded and gave his final approval. Now the only obstacle left in setting the departure date was the weather. From our only weather-related source, a portable AM radio, we listened each night to the Gerald Doyle newscast. When the weather forecast for the next day was "sunny with light winds," we decided that "this would be it," and we retired early to be well rested for the first leg of the trip. We awoke in the morning to a rainy, foggy, obviously unsuitable day and discovered that fifteen gallons of gasoline had leaked into the bilge. The reason became apparent and the necessary steps were taken to remedy the problem. After another even more encouraging weather forecast that evening, we scheduled our departure for the next day, Wednesday, July 22, 1953.

Day 1: July 22, 1953, Wednesday
Anchors Aweigh — St. Anthony, Newfoundland

The crew of the *Northern Messenger* awoke to a clear, bright, sunny day. Each person knew that, at last, we could allow this venerable ship to take us on one more of its many adventures. By 8:00 AM, we were ready; with Charlie, our captain at the helm, we motored out of the landlocked harbour of St. Anthony, past the lighthouse, and into the Atlantic. The northeast wind was light, not enough for setting the sails, so we stayed with the engine and headed north, up the picturesque coast, with "rodney" in tow (local name for a dinghy). John and I took turns at the wheel until we reached Quirpon (pronounced "car'poon"). Then Charlie guided the ship through the "tickle" (narrow passageway) where we felt the effects of the strong tidal current. At 11:45 AM, we set the course at 305 degrees that would take us across the northern tip of Newfoundland.

As we traveled along past Quirpon, we talked about the ancient mariners who may have sailed these same waters. At that time, we knew of the association of John Sebastian Cabot with Newfoundland, although his exact landings are in dispute. Local inhabitants even claimed he made landfall in this area, but they, like we, had no idea that we were looking at the very shore where a Viking settlement would be discovered in 1960—seven years after our journey. The site at L'Anse aux Meadows was occupied at least five hundred years before Cabot's explorations, and the archeological evidence shows that it was possibly primarily used as a repair place for their fleet of longboats.

Farther along our course as we passed Great Sacred Island, we saw the remains of a huge ship. It was years later that I learned she was the SS *Langleecrag*, a six-thousand-ton steamship that had just sailed from London, England, bound for Montreal. As the ship headed across the northern peninsula of Newfoundland on November 15, 1947, she came upon rain, fog, and heavy winds causing the crew to miscalculate their position. The helmsman apparently mistook the Cape Bauld light for the one at Cape Norman and incorrectly assumed they had cleared the tip of Newfoundland. He changed their course to the southwest, and at 5:30 AM, the SS *Langleecrag*, with crew of forty-three on board, was slammed against the rocks of Great Sacred Island; her 416-foot hull was snapped into two pieces, and the ship was a total loss. This fine steamship carried numerous depth finders, magnetic compasses, and radio transmitter/receiver. One member of the crew died, and the remaining men eventually were rescued from that bleak, deserted island. (I have often reflected on the fact that the *Northern Messenger* lacked all this equipment—except for a compass—and I marvel at our audacity to sail these same waters.)

[It was only after reading, *From Sled to Satellite: My Years with the Grenfell Mission*, authored by Dr. Thomas in 1987, that I learned what a key role he and the Grenfell Mission had played in the rescue and subsequent care of the survivors. In my years of working with him closely, he had never mentioned it. His book gives a fascinating account of the whole episode—his first notification in St. Anthony, boarding a whaling vessel for the harrowing trip to the site, the daring rescue by the whaler's crew, and the horrible stormy returning trip to St. Anthony for medical care and recovery of the forty-two men.]

As we motored along, blissfully enjoying the magnificent scenery on this cloudless day, we waved to the crew of the schooner *Minnie Maybury* headed east as we went west. We also saw, much farther away, the liner, SS *Samaria*. [In reviewing her history, I learned that she was a 19,730-ton steamship from the Cunard Line. Formerly a troopship during WWII, the six hundred-foot SS *Samaria* was used (in 1953 at the time of our sighting) as a cruise ship with a route from Liverpool, England, to Quebec. She could carry nine hundred passengers and crew. At the time we saw her in the Straits of Belle Isle, she had just been involved in the prestigious Fleet Review in Spithead, near Portsmouth, England, where the newly coronated Queen Elizabeth reviewed her naval fleet for the first time. Had we been able to communicate with the crew, one can imagine they were basking in the afterglow and excitement of that event.]

SS Samaria
(Courtesy of Railway Coastal Museum, St. John's)

John Jenkins in pilot house of Northern Messenger *(RML)*

We were abeam Cape Norman at 2:30 PM when a light northerly breeze stirred. We quickly took advantage of this opportunity to conserve our precious fuel and hoisted the main sail and two jibs. Unfortunately, the wind lasted only for an hour, so we struck the sails and restarted the engine. We were on course for Point Amour on the Labrador coast, about a mile from shore, when suddenly at 8:30 PM the engine sputtered and died. Out of the blue, three trap boats with fishermen, pulled alongside. Somewhat embarrassed, we willingly accepted their offer to tow us into Anse au Loup (pronounced locally, "Nancy Lou") where we dropped anchor. Immediately, there appeared two to three small boats with several blond, curly-headed young boys in each. They tied up to our boat, uttered nary a word, but gazed in amazement at what their dads had just dragged in. Meanwhile, the men worked over the slumbering engine and found the culprit—a burned-out coil. The source of the odor that we had detected all the way in was soon apparent—barrels of cod liver oil sat in the fishing sheds.

Towed in by trap boats to Anse au Loup, Labrador (RML)

In port at Anse au Loup visited by curiosity seekers (RML)

Quite unexpectedly—to us at least—the *Northern Ranger* dropped anchor about two hundred yards away. We were all familiar with this vessel that made regularly scheduled trips up and down both coasts of Newfoundland and the Labrador, carrying freight and passengers. These trips were curtailed each year from late fall until late spring due to the ice-bound harbours. We knew some of the crewmembers because of the many stops their ship had made at St. Anthony. During occasional layovers, when storms ruled the schedule, members from the mission staff and/or radar base officers would visit the ship for socialization—new faces and a respite from the isolation.

John, Charlie, and I rowed over to the ship in rodney. One purpose, besides delivering letters to be mailed, was to see if by some fluke they might have an extra coil on board to replace our faulty one. No luck on that score, but we did gratefully receive contributions for our larder—bread, canned meats, and fruits—straight from the engineer officers' pantry. We composed a note claiming to be ship-wrecked and pleading for help, that we placed in an empty ginger ale bottle. We asked Barry (*Northern Ranger*'s engineer), to deliver it to our skeptical friends at St. Anthony and tell them he found it bobbing around in the Gulf of St. Lawrence.

Northern Ranger *near Anse au Loup, Labrador*
(Courtesy of Railway Coastal Museum, St. John's)

The midnight row back to the *Northern Messenger* was unforgettable—no lights on land or sea to interfere with the awesome display above; the heavens filled with ghostly streaks of red and green and white, shimmering across the star-studded sky. When back on board with the rest of the crew, we reviewed the day and agreed that it had been most interesting and a great success—despite being towed in to shore and deposited on the Labrador coast in a less than elegant way—.

Day 2: July 23, 1953, Thursday
At Anchor — Anse au Loup, Labrador

The crew awakened early with one primary goal for the day—to find an electrical coil that would get that engine running again. Charlie set off on that mission in rodney and was told by the helpful fishermen on shore "the lighthouse keeper at Point Amour might have one." After his return with that good news, a fresh breeze developed at about 11:00 AM, so we hauled in the anchor and hoisted the mainsail and two jibs. They filled almost immediately, and we sailed out of the harbour at a pretty good clip. We were all elated to know that we would be saved a very long walk to Point Amour.

Our progress was short-lived, however, because once out of the harbour, our perfect wind died. With no engine and no wind, we drifted, and drifted, almost to Pinware, going many miles north of where we wanted to be—and moving in the opposite direction. The strong tide was pulling us close to the ledges, but each time, before we could panic, along came a small breeze that blew us out to safety.

All day long we were adrift. This could have been very boring if it weren't for the wildlife that gathered around us—birds, dolphins, and even a whale. Flying above us, we saw many Turr (a native bird of Newfoundland and Labrador) and the beautiful Puffins (Newfoundland's provincial bird) gathering in their orange beaks dozens of small fish. The dolphins were playful around the boat and followed us for most of the afternoon. Then for our further entertainment and delight, a sixteen- to eighteen-foot whale appeared, circling the boat several times. We held our breaths while he dove directly under the boat before finally waving good-bye with his tailfin as he swam away.

At 5:30 PM, we were jarred back to reality by a strong east-northeast wind that grabbed the sails and we were off again on the trail of that electrical coil that "might be" at Point Amour. We sped along smoothly, and at 8:00 PM dropped anchor at L'Anse au Mort. Charlie took off immediately to find the lighthouse keeper with the coil. When he returned, we could tell from his grin that he had success. Sure enough—not one, but *two!* Mr. Wyatt sold him one for three dollars and gave him another "as a gift." We saw yet another example of the generosity shown to us by these Newfoundlanders.

Charlie and John could hardly wait to install the newly acquired coil. While they worked on the engine, Marilyn and I rowed into shore to gather driftwood for our trusty woodstove. We enjoyed once more seeing the rustic beauty of the fishing stages (also called shanties). We were saddened to hear the men tell us of the tidal wave that had swept in there just before Christmas 1951—the worst storm they had ever seen. It destroyed one shanty after another—just like a row of dominos. They could be, and had been, rebuilt, but more devastating than that was the loss of equipment stored inside—fishing tackle, nets, barrels, engine parts, plus the small boats with their oars and other gear. All this was just swept out to sea along with the winter's supply of food for their dogs that had been stored in barrels in the fishing stages. It must have been a terrible time, but we could see evidence that these resilient people had rallied and somehow had been able to move forward.

As we left, our nostrils again reminded us that the industry here was cod and that codfish do have livers and that the livers produce the oil that we were told as children was just so good for us—and so tasty!

Charlie and John had installed the coil, gotten all the water out of the carburetor, cranked and cranked the sputtering engine until she finally produced the sound that was music to our ears. After finishing a hearty supper, at 10:00 PM, we pulled up the anchor and set our course for Forteau. There, we would visit the nursing station manned by Grenfell nurse-midwife, Lesley Diack, from England. Her district covered about forty miles of the coast, northeast to Red Bay and southwest to L'Anse au Claire. She is solely responsible for the medical (including obstetrical) needs of some 1,300 to 1,500 people.

The sky was dark and foreboding when, halfway across the bay, rain started pelting down. By 11:00 PM we had reached Forteau and dropped anchor (one of the small ones) near the lighthouse. We soon realized we were a little too close to the ledges to feel safe for the night. With rain still coming down, John and Charlie lifted the 150-pound anchor (kedge) into rodney, and the three of us rowed out a further distance from the shore, dragging the heavy anchor chain as we went. We had some difficulty getting the kedge up over the edge of the boat and into the water. The fluke caught on the gunnel and almost tipped us over. To use a Newfoundland expression, "It was some exciting!" Then it was back to the *Northern Messenger* to haul in some of the anchor chain in order to pull us further from shore.

We were all wide-awake after our harrowing—but successful—maneuver so at midnight Charlie, Peggy, Marilyn, and I rowed to the nursing station. (John stayed on board to stand watch on our vessel). Lesley greeted us warmly in spite of the late hour, and without any fanfare, produced hot coffee, berries, and other goodies seemingly out of nowhere. After the snacks, we took advantage of the opportunity to clean up with *warm* water before we left to go "home." We carried with us her donation of a washbasin for the ship. Then all of us hit the sack at 2:30 AM, except for Charlie who took the next four-hour watch. We calculated that day we had traveled about nine miles, as the crow flies, in eleven hours. (My log followed this with the Newfoundland expression—"shockin'!") All in all, it had been a good day with a happy ending.

Day 3: July 24, 1953, Friday
At Anchor — Forteau, Labrador

We were awakened at 8:15 AM by our onboard weatherman, John, with the discouraging report that the sky was overcast, winds were calm but a rapidly falling barometer—meaning that we would probably not be moving out today. Lesley Diack and Dorothy Tucker, another Grenfell worker, joined us for breakfast. Following a pleasant chat and their subsequent departure, I decided to row ashore to visit patients whom I had known at the hospital in St. Anthony. From Lesley's directions, I was able to find Eva Flynn with her mother and baby, Violet Flynn, Cora Hancock, Wilhelmina Hancock, and Mrs. Roberts. She sure was a sweetie and walked down to the fishing stage with me. When I asked her how she was doing, her answer was "I'm feelin' right smart, Miss." It was so good to see all these former patients doing so well and in their own homes.

When I arrived back at the boat, Marilyn greeted me with the dire news that the ship's custom papers and a key navigational chart were missing and that we might have to go back to St. Anthony for them in order to proceed south. After the glum crew tore the boat apart looking for them in vain, we all rowed ashore to the nursing station to cash in on our invitation for lunch but now with an even more important mission—to use the RT to locate the papers.

RT stood for radiotelephone—the only means of communication between the outlying nursing stations (six at the time) and the doctors (or staff) in St. Anthony. Each day at noon the nurses from all these stations called in to CJZ (zed) 30 (zero) and were connected with St. Anthony for the so-called "sched." This was their opportunity to get advice regarding particular patient-treatment problems and other concerns (e.g., arranging transportation for critically ill patients.) Calling at any time other than noon was nonproductive unless it had been prearranged.

On the dot of noon, Charlie used this method to call Audrey, the secretary in St. Anthony requesting that she search his former quarters in Sterling Cottage for the missing papers and chart. They agreed that she was to call back at 1:30 PM. We waited anxiously for her report and were so disappointed to hear that they were not there!

Charlie and John had planned to do their habitual tinkering with the engine upon returning to our boat but decided first to resume the search for the missing papers. Marilyn and I needed to get out of their way, and in order to relieve our own frustration, decided to try jigging for cod. We rowed out from the shore in rodney and dropped anchor. I was pretty skeptical but thought it was worth a try. I put the heavy, shiny lure on a fish line without any bait, dropped in the line, tugged up and down a few times and—*whammo!*—something hit, and I could barely pull up the line. When I finally did, a twenty-inch codfish was on the hook. I couldn't believe it. After deciding that there really *was* something to this jigging business, we kept at it until we had four beauties. We headed back to our boat, anxious to show the rest of the crew our catch and testify that this jigging method worked after all.

We were greeted with the fantastic news that Charlie had found the papers—but not the chart. After being duly praised for our fine catch, Marilyn and I delivered two of them to Lesley at the nursing station, who seemed very pleased to have some fresh cod for the staff's dinner. After learning the happy outcome of the missing papers saga, she contacted several of her fishermen friends who were able to produce just the chart we needed. It was far from the latest version, but we knew it was better than nothing at all.

By the time we were back on board the *Northern Messenger*, Charlie had cleaned our catch and was frying cod fillets and fish cakes for a celebration. We barely had finished our scrumptious dinner when the weather really kicked up and the rains came, and everything got wet. We even found a leak in our brand-new teakettle and, lastly, discovered we were out of water! The winds increased, forcing us in toward the rocky shore. Once again, we went into the mooring business, hauling two more anchors out in rodney and dropping them. When assured that they were holding, we continued into shore and visited the nursing station for a water supply. Lesley was able to give us a huge empty Klim can (powered milk container) and several smaller pails, which we filled and replenished our ship's tank.

The *Northern Messenger* was rolling like crazy but fortunately we were good seafaring sailors, except for Peggy who had been seasick whenever we were at sea and now, again, at anchor. We all retired at 12:15 AM, happy with plans and hopes that tomorrow we could sail across the straits to Flower's Cove, where we would be welcomed by Ivy Durley and the staff of another Grenfell station.

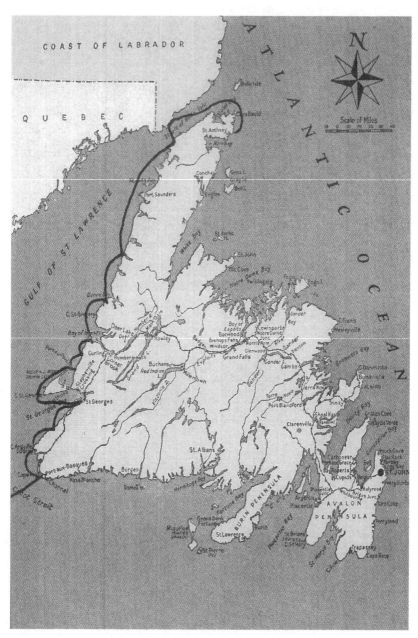

Newfoundland map showing partial route
followed by the Northern Messenger

Day 4: July 25, 1953, Saturday
At Anchor — Forteau, Labrador

We were awakened at 7:30 AM by the rolling of the ship. Wind and tide had set up a combination of continuous heavy rolling, pitching, and yawing motions. We were quite uncomfortable, to say the least; everything in the cabin seemed damp or wet. After breakfast, John and Charlie did their usual engine ritual while Marilyn and I whipped rope ends—and Peggy slept.

Peggy, Marilyn, and I rowed ashore to get *warm* baths at the nursing station, while Charlie and John continued to perform some more magic on the engine—tracing electrical circuits, taking the carburetor apart, and cleaning electrical contacts. Their efforts were rewarded; for the first time since 10:45 PM on Thursday (according to John's log), they heard that melodic purring of the engine.

That was indeed fortunate because by midday, John estimated that the wind had freshened to at least forty miles per hour out of the southwest with a wet steady drizzle. The ship rolled like crazy, and we were forced to move the anchorage again—but this time, *under motor power*—to a place above the nursing station in the lee of the hill, which provided more protection. During the move, rodney—being towed— got filled with water and sank. With great difficulty, we retrieved and bailed her out. The engine had at last performed heroically, and we all celebrated the men's achievement.

At 5:45 PM, the sky was beautiful with a whole range of red, yellow, and orange hues that we enjoyed as we rowed ashore for a six o'clock farewell dinner at Lesley's. We were embarrassed to find that the invitation was for five, not six.

They graciously had waited for their belated seafarers. Following the delightful meal, Lesley and I walked to Buckle Point where I met Lizzie's mother. (Lizzie was a nurse's aide at Forteau until she transferred to St. Anthony where I knew her).

From the station, we carried more water back to the ship; the men refueled the engine, and the crew retired at 11:30 PM after gazing at a beautiful full moon above. Our spirits had improved considerably since the morning.

We were all ready for an early morning departure toward our Boston destination, at last. We expected a sunny day with a perfect north wind and a calm sail back to the Newfoundland side of the straits.

Day 5: July 26, 1953, Sunday
At Sea — Crossing the Straits of Belle Isle

After Charles and John finished refueling and gazed at the lovely full moon while enjoying a light breeze, they decided that conditions were favorable enough to set sail immediately to cross the straits for the Newfoundland shore. That decision was bolstered by our AM radio's 11:00 PM Gerald Doyle weather report for Sunday—"warmer, sunny, and northerly winds."

We left our Forteau anchorage at 12:45 AM under mainsail and flying jib. We had planned to stow rodney on the deck for the crossing, but with our unexpected departure, there was no time, and she seemed fine bobbing along merrily astern on the smooth waters. At 3:40 AM, we were about two and half miles from shore and abeam the Flower Ledge light. A stop at Flower's Cove was no longer in our plans since we had already lost too many valuable days, so we sailed on through the night in a southerly direction and were greeted by a beautiful sunrise at 5:30 AM.

Just as John and I were preparing breakfast and finding it impossible to keep things stationary in the galley, the winds freshened. The water finally started to boil, and I said to John, "I don't think this pot will stay on the stove." Shortly after, during one mighty roll, John and I were thrown to the port side of the cabin; not only the pot but also the entire stove flew out, emptying its fiery contents on the galley deck. John grabbed the extinguisher and quickly got the fire under control. The entire cabin was a wet mess. Peggy was seasick and being tossed between the lower bunks along with her suitcase; papers and small items went flying from the wall racks.

The next five hours proved to be horrifying; the wind picked up and quickly reached thirty to forty miles per hour and veered more westerly all the time. John and Charlie inched their way out on the bowsprit to haul in the flying jib as the waves crashed over the bow. As we fell down into the troughs of the waves, their crests were higher than our mainmast.

Charlie and John struck the remaining mainsail, electing to rely on our trusty (?) engine. Just then, rodney's towline broke, and away she went. A dinghy, our only means to get to shore, was in the "essential" category. In these waters, there were very few docks or wharves, so our mooring would be at anchor 90 percent of the time. Determined that we must rescue her, Charlie turned the ship around with great difficulty and the *Northern Messenger* overtook rodney, unfortunately smashing into her with our bow. Hanging precariously over the gunnel, the men managed to tie another line on her, and we turned about and headed for the island in view. Rodney's towline snapped yet again, so we had to let her go this time. The wind was still about forty-five miles per hour, and we looked for lee anchorage behind the island with no exact idea of where we were. We dropped a grapnel, but it dragged in the muddy waters. John took soundings showing a depth of seven feet—just about our limit without going aground. We motored on to a deeper area and, at 10:30 AM, dropped in the kedge—the heaviest anchor we had—and all breathed a huge sigh of relief.

Two men soon came aboard from a trap boat, and we learned we were at Current Island and these men had sighted rodney with their binoculars. They assured us that they could bring her in and left immediately out into the still raging sea. Within an hour, they were back with rodney who was battered, torn, and leaking badly. We would have to deal with this problem later, and four of us retired to our bunks to try to sleep. Charlie chose to nap on deck to monitor the mooring. Most of the crew had been awake for about twenty-seven hours straight.

At 2:30 PM, a trap boat bumping against the hull awakened us, and who should appear, hopping up over the gunnel but the English nurse, Ivy Durley, who was in the area for a few days giving the annual inoculations to patients in her Flower's Cove district. She was a jolly person anyway, but to us, she was an angel who boosted our morale tremendously. She insisted that the three women go to shore with her to clean up and get some rest at "Aunt" Caroline's and that Charlie and John rest in their own bunks below, while two of her fisherman friends watched over the ship. No one had to be persuaded to follow her orders.

It was about 7:00 PM when Aunt Caroline served supper to the entire crew in front of a warm cozy fire. The fish chowder, bread, and berries were delicious. As the evening drew on, fifteen to twenty neighbors drifted in to see and hear the story about the seafarers who had chosen their island for refuge. Many had watched the whole episode from the shore, with baited breath, as they saw us struggle over the passageway that they knew had treacherous shoals.

We were taken back to the ship at 10:30 PM—except for Peggy who preferred to sleep in a stationary, dry bed at Aunt Caroline's—and thanked the hardy men who had been keeping watch. The wind was still high but nothing compared to the earlier hours. We listened to the Gerald Doyle Bulletin on our AM radio and learned that "there were *gales* in Newfoundland today." We all said in unison, "No kidding!" (My log read "Today we thought we had had it.") We soon went to our bunks for more of that needed sleep, confident that the worst of our trip was behind us—but it wasn't!

Day 6: July 27, 1953, Monday
At Anchor—Current Island, Newfoundland

This would be a day of rest, repair, and recovery for the crew of the *Northern Messenger*. We all had awakened at 10:30 AM—much later than usual—to happily find that the anchor was holding well, but the wind remained at twenty to thirty miles per hour. This, however, made little difference to us because neither we, nor the ship, were ready to sail today; so we enjoyed a leisurely breakfast with pancakes and fried corned beef, whipped up by our captain, Charlie. We all used another typical Newfoundland expression—it was "some good!"

In addition to the crew's need for a little relaxation after the experiences of the previous day, the ship too needed some TLC—a raft of things to be squared away before she could sail again. There was the general cleanup of the cabin, replacing and securing the wayward woodstove, airing and drying the wet clothing and sleeping bags, returning the items that had gone wandering to their rightful places, and pumping water from the bilge. Our gasoline, food, and water supplies needed to be replenished as well as the fire extinguishers.

It was crucial to get rodney on board ship in order to assess the damages and make repairs. Charlie and John had plenty of other jobs too—to secure the stern railing that had been pulled away by that second towline to rodney, to splice lines that had been torn apart, and to find another pair of oars on this island with a population of about eighty. Once rodney was brought on board, they found that, although she had a two- to three-inch hole in her port side and breaks in the gunnels, she could still be made seaworthy by a bit of patchwork and carpentry.

The day was filled with activity until we gladly welcomed aboard Ivy Durley at 4:00 PM. She brought her usual cheerful demeanor to our lives as she joined us for a pleasant—although sparse—supper. Sam Gibbons arrived in his trap boat at 9:30 PM to return Ivy to shore; Marilyn and John accompanied them in order to search for an essential replacement set of oars. They returned oarless but with some possible leads for a quest tomorrow. The four of us (Peggy was still enjoying the comforts at Aunt Caroline's) sat down and relaxed with a game of bridge. We had had a busy but enjoyable day, still anxious to move on to our next proposed stop—Port Saunders. We hit the bunks at about 12:30 AM, wondering what surprises the new day would hold.

[Current Island was established in the early 1800s as a seasonal fishing settlement with northern cod being the primary catch and salmon and herring to a lesser degree. I have been saddened to learn that in 1959, just six years after our visit when the population was about eighty, an epidemic of tuberculosis struck the island and almost all the residents were affected. By 1965, the island was abandoned.]

Day 7: July 28, 1953, Tuesday
At Anchor—Current Island, Newfoundland

Awakened by bright sunlight pouring into the cabin, the tone was set for a beautiful day. With the wind remaining at twenty to twenty-five miles per hour, even if we, the crew, had been foolhardy enough to brave the wind and the sea, the *Northern Messenger* was not ready to do so. Hence, John cooked up for us a great breakfast with oatmeal, Melba toast, fruit juice, and coffee. After discussing the plan for the day, we all got to work on our assigned tasks: the men repaired the dinghy, while Marilyn and I painted the table and unfinished parts of the deck. With those jobs done, it was time to eat again.

Charlie took his turn and brought forth a luscious lunch of spaghetti and meatballs. The day was progressing very well, but it was soon to become even better. Our jolly friend, Ivy Durley, appeared at two o'clock and invited us to ride over to Forrester's Point in the trap boat with her and Guy Gibbons. After a nice, smooth ride through the tickle, Guy delivered us to the mainland and left us to our own devices. All six of us including Peggy, all rested and recuperated, walked to Black Duck Cove for a most fascinating experience. We witnessed a family of three generations, readying their fish catch for marketing. The men in their oilskins gutted, washed, and dropped the fish into the brine, removed them with pointed wooden sticks, and loaded them on to a pony-driven two-wheel cart that the teenage boys guided to the beach. There, the women spread them out systematically on the flakes or rocks. Later, when dried from the sun, the small children collected them and piled them neatly in multilayer circles about two feet in diameter. When the whole process was finished, the dried collection of hundreds of fish was stored until needed or sold. We had just been privileged to see a demonstration of a smoothly run and harmonious family business.

Preparing fish—Black Duck Cove, Newfoundland (RML)

Horse drawn wagon carrying fish—
Black Duck Cove, Newfoundland (RML)

[Cod fishing was the only industry in the Great Northern Peninsula at that time—especially in these small isolated coastal towns. The waters were lovely fishing grounds that became quickly replenished despite being fished by hundreds of men in their small boats, but the number of fish began to dwindle with the invasion of larger trawlers that could travel faster, cover wider areas and fish at greater depths. Their radar, sonar, and electronic navigational systems made them no match for the smaller boats and local fishermen. By the summer of 1992, the northern cod population had dropped to 1 percent of its earlier peak level, putting an end to a five hundred-year industry. The Canadian government delayed taking action for reasons political and otherwise. Finally, in 1992, it declared a fishing moratorium in Newfoundland, but it was already too late. This, of course, was accompanied by great economic hardship throughout Newfoundland and Labrador as the province gradually had to find its way into other industries. This is a whole different chapter but with hopeful signs for a brighter future.]

Our hardy crew walked on to the small town of St. Barbe where we found a secluded area next to an inviting pool of water. Hot and tired from walking in this seventy-degree weather, Marilyn and John jumped in the pool in their long johns—shirts and all. With a little coaxing and daring, Ivy, not to be outdone, joined them in big bloomers and baggy shirt she had borrowed from Aunt Caroline. The water was icy cold, and the swim was brief. Nevertheless, I was able to memorialize the comical scene with my movie camera, while Ivy's protestations fell on deaf ears. It had been great fun and was topped off with a wonderful impromptu picnic on the beach by the lighthouse. Ivy, who knew and loved everyone in town and vice versa, scrounged from several households— and put together a supper of canned Newfoundland salmon (from the game warden), freshly-baked bread, rare cow's butter, berries, and tea—and we all agreed enthusiastically that it was "some delicious!"

[St. Barbe today has become an important location as the southern terminus for the ferry service to Blanc Sablon, Quebec, a short distance from Forteau where we were at anchor before our traumatic crossing of the straits. Today one may hop on the MV *Apollo* ferry, with her capacity of 240 passengers and seventy-five vehicles, and make the crossing in approximately one-and-three-fourth hours—although even now the schedule is "subject to change due to weather and ice conditions." Service is nonexistent (or curtailed) during the severe winter months. As of 1992, one could travel by car north on the Trans-Labrador Highway (TLH) as far as the Happy Valley Goose Bay area—and eventually beyond. The linkage to the Trans Canada transportation system at Blanc Sablon, Quebec, has brought profound changes in accessibility to the Labrador communities and their economy and industries.]

On our return walk, we stopped at a local store in Black Duck Cove to replenish a few groceries to the tune of $9.87. We then thanked Ivy for all the assistance and pleasure she had brought into our lives during these last few days, and sadly bid her good-bye.

We walked the two miles back to Forrester's Point while enjoying a shimmering sunset that turned the austere Anglican church from pure white to a lovely subdued pink and a cloud formation above that was threaded with streaks of gold. Just spectacular! We were able to hitch a ride with a fellow in his trap boat who steered us skillfully through the shoals of the tickle and back to our ship.

The crew was "some tired" that night and took to our bunks with the anticipation that we could at last sail tomorrow—*if the wind dies.*

Ivy, Marilyn, Charlie, John, and Peggy (RML)

Day 8: July 29, 1953, Wednesday
At Anchor—Current Island, Newfoundland

As the first member of the crew to awaken, I was greeted by the realization that the wind did *not* die. In fact, it was even higher than yesterday at thirty miles per hour out of the west-southwest. Since it looked like we were in for a wet, chilly day, I fired up the woodstove and prepared a nice brunch of corned beef hash, pickles, hot corn bread, and coffee. I have never been famous for my cooking skills, but I thought, *This isn't bad, if I do say so myself.*

Then we all settled down to work on more projects—Charlie patching the hole in rodney, John rehanging cupboard doors that fell off during the storm, Marilyn and I painting more of the deck and the life rings, and Peggy was still ashore at Aunt Caroline's.

By 3:30 PM, ready for some relaxation, John, Marilyn, and I rowed the rejuvenated rodney over to St. Barbe to fish in the beautiful salmon and trout streams that everyone had been raving about. On the way, we were able to pick up a pair of oars to replace those that had been lost. They were pretty chewed up but certainly would work well for us. We never did find those elusive streams, so there would be no salmon or trout for us tonight.

On the return from the swampy walk, we found an empty, rustic log cabin with no floor; we went inside and plopped ourselves down for a needed rest. John and Marilyn ate cold C rations right out of the can; I couldn't quite bring myself to do that. We stopped at the local store again and bought nails, eggs, tonic wine, and muffin mix—all for three dollars and seventy cents!

Our dinghy (rodney) lay on the beach at Forrester's Point where she was patiently waiting for our return. Once aboard, we struggled to row against the thirty-five to forty miles-per-hour wind; even with our newly acquired second set of oars, we just couldn't make any headway. It was 10:00 PM, and luckily, we found a young fellow in a trap boat who towed us back to our ship through the tricky shoals of the tickle. He and his garrulous uncle came aboard for a chat and a look-see. We all enjoyed coffee, strawberries, and thick sour cream and then off they went bearing our sincere "thank-you's" *and* our newly purchased bottle of tonic wine.

During the day, Peggy had returned from her shore leave, all rested up, saying she wanted to be all set and ready for our early morning departure. We had left St. Anthony a week ago and had covered one hundred miles with one thousand to go! (My log reads, "Shockin.")

Day 9: July 30, 1953, Thursday
At Anchor—Current Island, Newfoundland

So much for an early departure, the day was overcast with intermittent rain and a west-southwest wind of twenty to thirty miles per hour. *No sailing today!*

Marilyn attempted to lift our spirits with a scrumptious breakfast of scrambled eggs, fried baloney, date-nut bran muffins, and coffee. It bolstered our spirits a little but not completely.

We heard the putt-putt of a trap boat, and we welcomed aboard Doug Gibbons and his baby girl. After he had proudly shown us the baby, we all got in his boat to spend the rest of the day ashore.

Interwoven among numerous pleasant chats over tea during the day with friends and neighbors of Aunt Caroline and Uncle George were the crew's assigned tasks. After hauling water from the pond to a barrel, Marilyn and I did a huge load of everyone's wash and hung it on the picket fence to dry, followed by shampooing our hair in the frigid pond. Charlie and I then rowed their dinghy to a spring where we could get water for our ship's tank and gather some wood for the stove. The return row against the wind was "some tough."

The day had been a refreshing and delightful change, and when it was time to go, George Gibbons took us back to the ship and climbed aboard.

While Charlie and I prepared supper of macaroni and cheese, we listened intently to George's tales, gleaned from years of experience fishing and sailing these straits. He told us of strong tides, dangerous tide rips, unique wind effects on the waves, nearby ship wrecks, and more—which was enough to reinforce our respect for these fishermen and our own awareness of the hazards. The gist of his final message to us was "stay the hell out of the straits in small boats during west and southerly winds!"

Following Guy's entertaining but interesting visit, we listened to the AM radio weather report: "Small craft warnings in the straits today. Wind to shift to northwest at fifteen miles per hour tomorrow." This didn't quite gibe with our barometer reading that was steady at 29.08 millibars. We prayed that the forecast was correct because we intended to make the six-hour run to Port Saunders in the morning. The entire crew was restless and increasingly concerned about meeting its individual deadlines. We hit the bunks at 12:30 AM ready and anxious to get back to the sea and find what other interesting adventures would develop.

Day 10: July 31, 1953, Friday
At Anchor—Current Island, Newfoundland

Yes, you are reading the title above correctly; we were *still* at Current Island! The forecast was *not* correct, and it's no wonder; we learned that it actually comes from St. John's, some five hundred to six hundred miles to the southeast as the crow flies. Quite a different part of the world! There was no chance of moving out until the wind had abated.

Marilyn cooked a delicious breakfast of oatmeal, Spam, orange juice, toast, and coffee. There were always optional chores to be done while we waited for the elusive "wind shift to northwest fifteen miles per hour" that was forecast last night. Marilyn painted more of the deck; I painted the wheelhouse while the men found plenty else to do. Charlie did the lettering on the life rings and said when he got as far as *Northern Mess* . . . he almost left it at that. Our ship is really beginning to look "smart." (Newfoundland term for "good" or "great.")

Our outing for the day was a row in the dinghy to Sheep Island, where we were told we would find lots of "plum boy" berries and maybe bakeapples (a native berry found in arctic and alpine tundra—*Rubus chamaemorus*). After searching high and low, we calculated that we had averaged about twenty per person, most of which we had quickly eaten. But the trip was not a disappointment; we found a lovely field of wildflowers where we just lay in the soft grass watching the beautiful, puffy white clouds urgently rolling by as if they had places to go.

We were back aboard the ship by 5:00 PM after our delightful berry-picking expedition. The menu for supper was unique—bottled rabbit given to us by Guy's brother, Doug, hot sliced pineapple, mashed potatoes, and chocolate pudding. It was my first taste of rabbit, but it was surprisingly appealing.

Guy and Doug later arrived bearing gifts for tomorrow's breakfast— thirty to forty capelins (small fish similar to smelt). Lots of genial conversation and their jokes that we should be able to make Boston by *Christmas!* We were beginning to think they were not far wrong.

Another trap boat bumped against the ship bringing more visitors for tea and a nice visit—Aunt Caroline, Uncle George, and Mr. Toope. Such wonderful people, like so many others, who have made this week of frustrating delay turn into a wonderful, heartwarming interlude by their generosity and concern for our well-being.

By 11:00 PM, the wind had dropped to a flat calm, but the radio forecast still was "northwest wind around twenty miles per hour." It looked more likely that we might be saying final good-byes to our good friends on Current Island tomorrow. My log reads, "I think tomorrow will be the day!"

Leaving Current Island, Newfoundland (RML)

Day 11: August 1, 1953, Saturday
Anchors Aweigh — Current Island, Newfoundland

"Today *was* the day all right!" reads my log. There was a beautiful calm sea greeting us in the morning. We had a quick breakfast of Guy's dried capelin, and as instructed, we just fried them right on the bare top of the stove. They were okay, but we wouldn't want them as a steady diet, and we didn't seem to mind that you eat the entire fish—*head and all.*

We lost no time in hoisting the anchor to be piloted through the shoals by Sam and Guy Gibbons. Once out of the harbour, we charted our course for 250 degrees and set the main and mizzen sails and had a beautiful run. As we passed abeam Ferrole Point at 10:22 AM, we sighted the SS *Springdale* about eight miles away. At 2:15 PM, we turned on the engine for even more power, and we really moved along. We were getting such good speed we thought we could go beyond Port Saunders—maybe even to Bonne Bay—but at 7:30 PM, we realized we hadn't yet seen the Cowhead light.

Then the rains came down; the sails flapped idly as we searched for the Cowhead light. We finally found it, set way back in the rugged cliff. We thought that the placement was rather dumb. At 8:00 PM, we lowered the main sail and started to motor into the harbour amid the rain and swells when the motor suddenly stopped. This time, water had gotten into the gas line. Charlie and John rectified the situation after two hours of trying all their tricks, and the engine started again. It wasn't easy refueling from the 350-pound drum that was lashed to our deck.

It was foggy and still raining when the engine stopped again—this time overheated—and just would not start again. We hoisted the mainsail, and with a light breeze, we finally arrived at the southerly side of the harbour where we dropped anchor in two fathoms of water at 11:00 PM.

It was such a great relief to finally be at anchor and in front of our warm and toasty woodstove. We all were exhausted. We hadn't eaten much during the day, so Charlie produced a variety of soups—tomato, chicken, and vegetable—and hot rolls. We devoured them all.

Marilyn and John were on watch until 3:30 AM when I relieved them. The sky was beautiful, filled with glistening stars, hardly any lights on the ground to distract from their beauty.

Day 12: August 2, 1953, Sunday
At Anchor — Cowhead, Newfoundland

Charlie got up at 6:00 AM to do some tinkering on the engine, so I took a nap until 10:30 AM. Everything was in good order by 8:10 AM when the crew hauled in the anchor, turned on the engine, and we were again at sea with a nice north northwest breeze of fifteen miles per hour. At about two miles from shore, we raised the mainsail and zipped right along under sail and engine. We were abeam the beautiful Lobster Cove lighthouse at about 2:30 PM. (It was built in 1897 and still stands as an example of a well-proportioned, functional tower as they were at the beginning of the twentieth century.)

This was one of our most picturesque and uneventful sailing days. We viewed the beautiful, steep cliffs around us as we approached Bonne Bay. To add to our viewing pleasure, we saw a Marconi-rigged ketch with her sails full, so pretty against the gray cliffs and the cumulus clouds. John's log read, "Breathtaking and surpassing our expectations."

Northern Messenger *in Bonne Bay, Newfoundland (RML)*

We tied up to Butt's Wharf at Woody Point at 2:30 PM, pleased with such an early arrival. With such magnificent scenery all around us, we felt it would be appropriate not only to tidy up the ship but ourselves as well. I gave haircuts to John and Charlie before they washed up and got into their best clothes. Meanwhile, below deck, Marilyn and Peggy were doing the same thing and donning skirts and sweaters.

Off the ship and up the street we all went in our finery, expecting to find a nice restaurant to welcome us on this occasion, and where people would admire—or at least notice—our now smartly dressed selves. Our only success came when a Mrs. Crocker, at an establishment similar to a bed and breakfast, took us in, even though the sign said *Closed*. The price was right at one dollar a piece, but the quantity of food hardly filled our empty stomachs. Rather than explore further, back to the ship we went, and Charlie prepared shepherd's pie, fresh berries (from Sheep Island), and Jell-O. Then we all felt so much better.

We noticed hundreds of fish under our boat and decided to take advantage of this situation. We had no real bait, so we tried pieces of rolls and cheese first; after we caught a couple, we used the eyes. Then the fish below took to the bait so fast that we continued to use eyes until we had caught a dozen good-sized cod. Charlie and I cleaned them to have them ready for a meal the next day.

This was the first time that we had enjoyed the luxury of being tied up to a wharf instead of being anchored. We took advantage of it and left our ship several times for hiking, rowing, or just plain exploring this beautiful area. The towering cliffs above the fjord, that had been carved out of a glacier, waterfalls, and little fishing villages, made for exquisite scenery. A most enjoyable day!

[In 2005, the area was designated Gros Morne National Park—the second largest in the Atlantic Canadian provinces. Today, with a main highway running up the coast, it is a popular tourist attraction.]

Peggy and Charlie near Bonne Bay, Newfoundland (RML)

Day 13: August 3, 1953, Monday
Butt's Wharf — Woody Point, Newfoundland

Woody Point was just the place we needed for the day to fulfill our various supply needs—Charlie and John shopped for such things as gasoline, packing grease for the engine, paint, nails and a half-inch line. We three females stocked the food larder (located under the bunks) and shopped for other sundries. I bought a pair of loafers for $4.50.

For the first time, we were near a telegraph office, so each of us had messages to send. We found places for lunch in town, and for the first time, we had some ice cream—Brookfield at that!

Marilyn and John went over to Mr. Butt's bungalow and, after a delightful chat, were able to bring back plenty of water for the ship's tank. Marilyn and I cooked up a supper of potatoes, sausages, apple rings, cabbage and tomato salad, strawberries, and cream.

John then left on the ferry to Neddie's Point where he could get medical attention for his ear. He met members of a wedding party who were headed for a dance and reception. They invited all the crew of the *Northern Messenger* to attend. Meanwhile at the wharf, we were concerned when John didn't appear by 8:00 PM. Charlie, Marilyn, and I were going to row the mile and a half to find him, but we were saved the trip when a helpful townsperson with a special phone was able to call the hospital and learn that he had already left. By the time we had returned to the ship, he was already there—feeling very happy. He and Marilyn decided to accept the invitation to the dance and left the ship at 11:00 PM, rowing our dinghy the one and a half miles to Neddie's Point.

Since we were hoping to sail at 6:00 AM, we three party poopers hoped they would find their way back safely and in time for the early departure. Before hitting my bunk at twelve, I celebrated with the rare Coca-Cola that I was so happy to find that day. It tasted like a million bucks! The absent couple arrived about 3:00 AM, having gotten a tow back from Neddie's Point with a newly acquired friend from the wedding party, Clyde Reed. They were feeling no pain.

Day 14: August 4, 1953, Tuesday
Butt's Wharf — Woody Point, Newfoundland

The sky was overcast when we all awoke at 7:00 AM, and intermittent rain showers were present. We cleared the wharf by 9:00 AM. As we motored away from the breathtaking panorama of Bonne Bay, we kept close to the high cliffs because we knew the water there was very deep; the sun came out, the wind freshened, and we hoisted the mainsail and flying jib. It seemed like we were, indeed, *flying* as we passed Eastern Head by 9:50 AM and were abeam Skinner's Cove at 10:20 AM. The *Northern Messenger* was sailing like a charm under just perfect wind conditions for us. We were making five and a half knots. *It seemed almost too good to be true!*

Sure enough, it was. The wind dropped at 1:45 PM, so we struck the sails after a tack that brought us too close to a dangerous shoal near St. Gregory, merely three boat lengths away! Only by a 90 degree rapid change of course did we avoid it.

We entered the Bay of Islands at 2:00 PM under motor alone until it cut out at 2:50 PM. This time, the belt for the generator and water pump broke. At a most favorable time for us, the wind freshened; we hoisted the mainsail, mizzen and flying jib, and made beautiful time through the stunning bay. We saw Frenchman's Head at 4:50 PM while still making five and a half knots, then passed abeam Meer Point at 5:55 PM. We sailed in to the Western Terminal Wharf at a pretty good clip, but the crew was able to handle the maneuver skillfully without mishap (thank goodness), and we were all tied up by 7:30 PM. We knew that a friend, Ann Whitehurst, who had worked in St. Anthony, was visiting at her home in Corner Brook. We called her from a phone on the dock (first one we had seen in a long time). She and her father drove down to pick us up in his snazzy Cadillac. On the way to their home, he showed us his rather posh country club (now known as the Blomindon Golf and Country Club) and its spectacular views of the Blow Me Down Mountains.

It felt so strange to be in a metropolis— relative to Current Island, that is. (The population of Corner Brook at that time was thirteen to fourteen thousand.)

We had a pleasant evening at the Whitehurst home, especially enjoying their delicious ice cream smothered with fresh smashed strawberries. They drove us back to our ship at 11:45 PM. It was difficult for the crew to fall asleep after the excitement of the past two days, so we chatted from our bunks until one by one, we fell asleep, and then there was silence.

Day 15: August 5, 1953, Wednesday
Western Terminal Wharf —
Corner Brook, Newfoundland

I was up and raring to go by 8:00 AM and was surprised to learn that John already was ashore in search of eggs for our breakfast. He came back empty-handed with the sad news that the stores were not yet open, so we settled for coffee and hard rolls.

Ann arrived at 9:30 AM; Peggy and Marilyn went ashore with her for some shopping. I stayed on board while Charlie and John went to check in with the customs agent. With that business out of the way, they asked for help in finding a mechanic. He recommended a Mr. Noseworthy, whom they later found at the Newfoundland Tractor Company. Once there, they were able to purchase wrenches and spare parts for our engine. They also tried to locate a current navigational chart for the waters between Codroy and Sydney, Nova Scotia, but none was to be found.

We all were driven by Ann to the Whitehurst home where we were treated royally to a dinner of roast beef, fresh peas, potatoes, Yorkshire pudding, apple pie, and ice cream. We could find no words to describe how wonderful that dinner was to our taste buds as well as psyches.

Ann took us back to the ship, and we bade her good-bye. Mr. Noseworthy had returned with Charlie and John to clean the carburetor and tune up the engine. They worked on the antiquated engine until it finally was purring smoothly.

The weather was calm with light showers, and we felt it was good enough to cast off the lines at 5:10 PM and head for Larke Harbour.

Under power, we were abeam Meer's Point by 6:10 PM and Frenchman's Cove by 6:45 PM. We entered Larke Harbour (twenty-six miles from Corner Brook) and tied up to a schooner at the wharf by 8:15 PM. Marilyn and John prepared a delicious dinner of hamburgers, potatoes, and cake. We were told by one of the schooner's crew members that an urgent message had been broadcast on the Gerald Doyle Bulletin program asking us to contact somebody immediately (but they couldn't remember who!). Charlie and John walked a mile to the telegraph office, in the rain and under heavily overcast sky, and sent a wire to Gerald Doyle to get the true gist of the bulletin's message. Meanwhile, Peggy and I were enjoying singing songs as Marilyn sang and played her guitar.

The men arrived back from their arduous task at 10:30 PM with the news that their new message would not be delivered until the next morning. This meant that we would have to wait until the telegraph office opened in the morning at nine before we could possibly get any reply. This was very disappointing and impractical because we would need an early start for tomorrow's long run.

We retired at 11:00 PM after discussing the plan for tomorrow, knowing that due to the almighty weather in this part of the world, plans are often put on hold, modified, or cancelled. We didn't know which it would be or did we have any idea that it was to be the most terrifying day of our lives.

Day 16: August 6, 1953, Thursday
Tied to Schooner — Larke Harbour, Newfoundland

This momentous day started at 5:30 AM when we were abruptly awakened by the skipper of the schooner to which we were tied, who told us that they were pulling out. After the schooner cleared the area, we motored into their spot and tied up once more.

After a quick breakfast, Marilyn and I walked to the telegraph office a mile away just in case it had opened early and were so disappointed to find it closed. We decided not to wait and left a note requesting that our messages be forwarded to Cape St. George and also one to be sent to Charlie's wife, in Boston, who was awaiting the delivery of her first child. (Not one of these was ever received.) The weather was overcast and cool, and it was difficult to judge the wind speed in this sheltered harbour, but feeling an increasing sense of urgency to proceed with our trip, we left Larke Harbour at 7:45 AM in intermittent rain and fog. After clearing Shag Island, we hoisted the mainsail and working jib. Just as we were clearing Long Point, about 1:00 PM, the wind freshened and changed from west-northwest to northwest. The sky was overcast. Normally, those blue patches in the sky would be harbingers of good weather to follow but not so this time. The seas began to mount, the wind increased to more than forty miles per hour, the ship rolled, and we were carried into the deep troughs of the waves, which were higher than the mast. We struggled to strike the jib and put a reef in the mainsail; we had to use the motor to assist in the steering. Many times we were hit by the gigantic waves from the side during some mighty rolls. The waves slammed over the bow and attempted to remove everything that was loose. Rodney fortunately stayed on board as we had lashed her securely upside down. The 350-pound drum of gasoline that had been attached to the main mast was carried overboard and lost forever; a loose grapnel anchor smashed into the head hatch leaving a gaping hole. Down in the cabin, the woodstove was thrown out once more onto the galley deck.

ADVENTURES OF A GRENFELL NURSE

The winds were still increasing when we sighted, off in the distance about ten miles away, an island, later identified as Red Island. We headed for refuge in its lee but were making very poor time, enduring five punishing hours battling the sea with huge waves still crashing over the bow before finally reaching the small island. All we could see were the steep, gray, unfriendly cliffs of the mainland as we dropped the 150-pound kedge anchor at 6:00 PM. The sandy bottom made poor holding ground. The crosswind caused very rough riding. The anchor was dragging, and we were heading toward the cliffs. Finally, we felt the anchor grab when we were no more than a hundred yards from the cliffs. Although we were unsure of the water depth, it was some consolation to assume that now all we had to do was ride out the storm. How wrong we were!

We thought that at last we could feed our weary bodies. First thing that greeted us as we went down the hatch to the galley was the woodstove strewn all over the galley deck again. We got it back in place, and Marilyn, John, and I tried to prepare supper. The ship was rocking so much that John had to go up to the stern deck and attach a line from a post to a grapnel anchor and throw it in to help keep the bow of the ship into the wind. This worked for only a few minutes before tearing loose and allowing that anchor to sink to the bottom.

Starting the fire was difficult with wet wood, but finally it was blazing. As we continued to prepare supper, we could hear loud banging sounds as the ship was yanked against the anchor chain with each wave. Soon pots and pans were flying out of their designated places and onto the deck.

The ship was still rolling, and eventually, just as the pot of water was boiling, it toppled over, and we started all over again. When the macaroni was almost done, the ship took one tremendous lurch and the pot—macaroni and all—splattered to the deck.

At 10:30 PM, we gave up on the hot supper idea, and three of us tried to get some sleep, leaving John and Marilyn on watch in the wheelhouse, but there was no sleep to be had. At 11:00 PM, with the storm still raging and the ship rolling worse than ever, the second grapnel attached to the stern just wrenched away the entire railing and sank to the bottom of the sea. At 11:30 PM, there was a dreadful loud explosive sound. *The main anchor chain had just broken*, sinking to the bottom attached to the kedge and taking away our last means of remaining in one spot.

All hands quickly got to the deck, realizing the dire situation. The only thing we could see as we looked toward the shore in the inky darkness were the white crests of the waves crashing against those steep cliffs, and we were being pushed nearer and nearer to them by the northwest wind—now at forty-five plus miles per hour. We all quickly donned our life jackets as Charlie and John struggled to start the engine.

The crew had previously discussed the fact that our chart showed a sandbar extending all the way from the shore to Red Island with water depth of seven feet at high tide (our draft was exactly seven feet). The only way we could get out to the open sea safely to avoid that obstacle was to go around the north side of the island (*and into the wind!*) Charlie and John worked and worked on the engine, begging it to start, but it would only bark and sputter, as if to say "I got you here, didn't I? I've done my work for the day." Marilyn and I threw out still another grapnel, which slowed us down a little, but that too was dragging. As Charlie continued working on the stubborn engine, John, Marilyn, and I raised the mainsail with great difficulty and attempted to head us into the wind to take us north around the island. We couldn't make any headway. The wind was just too strong, the seas too high, and the ship was being blown toward the cliffs. We were no more than thirty feet from them when John yelled to Charlie, *"Get up here, now!"* He rushed up from the engine room, not knowing what he was going to find. He quickly assessed the situation, grabbed the wheel, but had no better results than we at heading into the wind. So he quickly spun the wheel 180 degrees to jibe. We ducked our heads as we came about, and the mainsail and its heavy boom swung around with great fury. We were then headed south, going with the strong wind. We braced ourselves, knowing that we should be hitting the sandbar soon. As we passed over it, we felt the keel graze the bottom but the ship continued on. It must have been high tide because the crest of the wave carried us right over the sandbar and we were free and away from those horrifying cliffs. What a relief!

Now, at midnight, we had no choice; we were out in the strong sea again, anchorless, and motorless—but we had the sails, and at least we were heading *south!*

Day 17: August 7, 1953, Friday
At Sea — Red Island to St. George's Bay, Newfoundland

The waves still seemed mountainous, even higher than before, as we headed for Cape St. George. At 2:45 AM, we rounded the cape, and then the wind started dropping; by dawn, it was almost flat. The night was black with no lights to be seen until we sighted the beacon from Harmon Airfield in Stephenville, and we followed it into St. George's Bay. During this time, Charlie and I took turns at the wheel while the others tried to sleep. Marilyn and John relieved us at 7:00 AM, and we were abeam Isthmus Bay at 9:10 AM; and by 11:45 AM, we tied up at the government wharf on Flat Island.

Greatly relieved to be alive with ship intact—*well almost*—we all tried to get some sleep and rested until the middle of the afternoon when we each had plenty of assignments awaiting us. Charlie and John were able to track down two tractor tires to be used as fenders at the wharf, and they also luckily found another kedge anchor. Just to get some relaxation before tackling their jobs, Marilyn and John went for a walk— she with her binoculars to find some native birds, and John with his camera to record the local environs. Peggy and I got a ride in a trap boat to cross the bay for replenishing some of our food supplies. We were lucky to find sailmaker's needles with which we could mend our tattered sails.

Everyone stayed on board for supper that night. Neither John's log nor mine even mentioned what the menu was. I guess it really didn't matter that much. I do remember that it included wine. Marilyn brought out her water-soaked guitar for a sing-along. We were all thankful to have survived the events of the day and so happy to have left Red Island far behind. John wrote in his log: "Peggy seems dispirited." This was an understatement. Following this episode, Peggy made arrangements to fly home. We all hit the sack at 10:30 PM for a good night's sleep with the *Northern Messenger* tied securely to the dock.

Day 18: August 8, 1953, Saturday
Government Wharf — Flat Island, Newfoundland

The west wind is fifteen to twenty miles per hour this morning contributing to the minor mishap, which started the day. John discovered early in the morning that the *Northern Messenger*'s bowsprit was hooked on the dock and cracking with the tide going down. He woke Charlie, and together they were able to pivot the ship around to remedy the problem before any more damage could be done.

A group of friendly mariners gathered around the ship to take a look at the damage. They had lots of reliable, specific advice as to whom and where we needed to go to solve many of the problems. John's log contained a detailed list entitled "Survey of Storm Damage":

> Bobstay carried away; life ring carried away; stern rail wrenched loose from bulwarks and twisted out of shape; fuel drum and 20–25 gallons gas lost; masthead light dangling and glass broken; 150 pound kedge anchor and 12 fathom (72 feet) of anchor chain lost; port in head hatch broken; two rents in mainsail at reef points; boltrope gone near first reef point; leach gave at the seam; smashed outer flange, which was carried away, on portside hawse; one axe missing; stove adrift, grate broken but splinted together.

There were jobs for everyone that day. Marilyn and I (with help from the men) unlashed rodney and guided her down into the water. We rowed away from the wharf to a spot where we hoped to find some driftwood for the stove, and coincidentally, a secluded place where we could wash up. Both tasks were accomplished, and we rowed back against the stiff west wind and learned that one of Charlie's and John's new friends had invited our crew to lunch. The entire Coulson family was anxious to hear the saga of our trip from Red Island to Flat Island.

We came away with lots of helpful, friendly tips that would facilitate getting on with the trip as soon as possible.

After the nice lunch, we all resumed our assigned tasks—John went ashore in search of another drum of gasoline, Marilyn and Charlie sewed the tatters in the sail, Peggy went for a walk to get information regarding her travel options to Toronto, and I was gathering and chopping more wood christening the new axe we had just purchased.

During the remaining afternoon, Charlie and John were busy repairing various damages and also, of course, working on the engine. They finally got it started after three or four cranks and John is quoted in his log as saying, "Seems we should not depend on it for emergencies. Ship handles better in rough seas and wind under sail."

It was my turn to prepare supper, and when I opened the larder (compartment under one of the bunks), what a *disaster* I found. All the labels from the canned goods were wet and strewn everywhere. *Not a single can could be identified!* Apparently, during the previous day's storm, when we were taking on lots of water, this area was full and the cans were merrily sloshing around. (We had pumped the bilge many times during the storm, but obviously, that didn't prevent this troublesome situation.)

I planned to serve canned salmon, potatoes, and peas for our dinner. When I opened the can that had the appropriate shape, I uncovered a strange dark meat that was definitely not salmon. Upon further review and discussion with the crew, we identified it as the *seal meat* that we had been given by Guy Gibbons on Current Island. From that dinner forward, we never dared to announce the menu in advance. The surprising combinations were often humorous but never was a meal turned down.

We were all dead beat that evening, but Marilyn was more than tired. At 10:00 PM, her temperature was 100.8 degrees Fahrenheit. As the only nurse on board, I had packed a kit with first aid and other medical supplies, and I gave my patient some aspirin with codeine as a starter.

The crew retired at 11:00 PM after a tiring full day with evidence of having made much progress. Charlie chose to take the first watch due to gusty onshore west-southwest winds with the danger of the bowsprit getting hooked again on the wharf. John relieved him at 3:30 AM.

Day 19: August 9, 1953, Sunday
Government Wharf — Flat Island, Newfoundland

On this day, the sun rose at 6:20 AM with scattered clouds and a wind speed of twenty miles per hour out of the southwest. The change in wind direction was good news but not the speed of twenty.

The two tractor tires provided by Mr. Coulson had broken loose due to the pounding of the ship against the dock during the night. Later in the morning, John decided to go out in the dinghy and try to retrieve them. He had heard about some anchor chain that had been lost off a government barge last winter and thought maybe he could find that at the same time and save us some money. We needed to replace the seventy-two feet of chain that we had lost on the bottom near Red Island. No such luck! He found the site, all right, and was able to hook it with the gaff, but he just couldn't pull it up; the weight was too great. After he failed at the anchor chain project, he sighted a huge lobster. He tried and tried to catch him with the gaff, but the creature was too clever and slithered away. *There goes my dream of a lobster dinner tonight,* he thought.

Repairs were getting completed, supplies were being replenished and another kedge acquired, but it was still a "down" day for the crew. Marilyn was sick with a fever of 102.4 degrees Fahrenheit. I stayed aboard with her while the others went to the Coulson's again to experience a new taste thrill —moose meat. They reported that it was *delicious.*

During the afternoon, John had a meeting with Mr. Sharon from the air force base in Stephenville. They needed to synchronize the date of his termination from the corps of engineers with his entrance date to medical school at Dalhousie in Halifax. Peggy made her reservations to fly TCA (Trans-Canada Airline) from Stephenville tomorrow, Marilyn slept, and I took a row in the dinghy to collect some more firewood. Charlie probably worked on the engine.

We all appreciated the supper prepared by Peggy of chicken soup, pineapple, peach turnovers, and coffee—especially the turnovers. John found special pleasure from the beer he brought back from shore because its availability has been almost nonexistent. Everyone was ready to turn in by 10:00 PM still feeling the effects of Thursday and Friday's stressful journey.

Day 20: August 10, 1953, Monday
Government Wharf — Flat Island, Newfoundland

All the crew members were itching to get on with our trip for different reasons—Charlie, in order to reach home in Boston before the birth of his first baby; John, for his starting date at medical school in Halifax; Peggy and Marilyn, to make connections for their trips home; and I, to catch the northbound steamer in Port aux Basques to return to my position in St. Anthony for another year.

We had all become resigned to the fact that we would not be sailing the *Northern Messenger* to Boston as originally planned; our goal now was to reach North Sydney, Nova Scotia, by August 18.

We awoke this Monday morning with a sense of urgency to depart while the weather seemed so favorable. Although the wind was flat at 5:30 AM, it had increased to ten miles per hour by 8:00 AM—the velocity we could easily handle.

After eating our breakfast of porridge, toast, fried Spam, fruit juice, and coffee, Charlie and John found Mr. Coulson and returned to him his two tractor tires. They shook hands and reluctantly said good-bye. He had undoubtedly been of great help to us during the stay at Flat Island.

We cast off the dock lines at 8:45 AM and motored across to St. George's to pick up a few groceries but, more importantly, gasoline as we had only enough on board for a three to four-hour run. After a thorough search of possible sources, we had absolutely no luck. We would have to leave without it and trust the wind and engine to cooperate with us a little —just for a change.

We left St. George's at 10:30 AM and saw the Sandy Point beacon at 10:45 AM where we raised the mizzen, main, and working jib and cut the engine to save gas. We were sailing close-hauled into the fifteen-miles per hour wind. We lashed down anchors and anything else that might wander and prepared for a long run. All went well, allowing some of the crew to catch up on still needed rest, *until the wind died*, forcing us to turn on the engine.

We reached Robinson's Head at 4:00 PM when, suddenly, both the engine and the wind died. We knew there was plenty of water beneath us, so we relaxed and Marilyn prepared supper of creamed salmon, rice, and waxed beans that just seemed to hit the spot. Meanwhile our sails were slatting loosely all evening while we were in the vicinity of Gull's Nest Rock.

We had no choice but to stay put and keep watch through the night for shoals or hazards. The weather was clear with no wind, and we were treated to a spectacular display of shimmering streaks of red and blue and gold across the heavens. Peggy and Charlie took the first watch while the rest of us slept. When my turn came at 11:00 PM, we were just drifting around in circles.

Day 21: August 11, 1953, Tuesday
Adrift near Gull's Nest Rock, Newfoundland

I saw lots of fish swimming under the boat. So to break the monotony, I put out the jigging line. Within minutes, I hauled in two beauties, each about twenty-four inches long. At 2:00 AM, we fried one of them and had cod steaks for a nice treat. *Some good!*

At 3:00 AM, Marilyn gave me a haircut, and I took to my bunk from 4:00 to 8:30 AM. By then the wind had been just strong enough to move us on toward Wreck Cove (we really didn't care for the name at that point). Charlie and John tried one last trick to start the engine; they drained the small amount of remaining gas from the starboard tank and mixed it with the poor gas from the port tank (which had a little water in it). They were able to get the engine started for a period long enough to carry us to the Cape Anguille lighthouse by 1:45 PM, and then it quit. We were able to work our way in toward Codroy during the afternoon under sail but with very little wind until we were three quarters of a mile from shore. John, Marilyn, and I rowed the dinghy in through the fog and rain to the refuge of the lighthouse at 6:00 PM. As we approached the shore, we fantasized that the lighthouse keeper would invite us in for a turkey dinner and hot baths. He didn't, of course, but being a generous Newfoundlander, Gus Patey, did give us five gallons of gas, which would be fuel enough to take us in to Codroy.

We delivered the precious cargo to our delighted captain, Charlie. We, in turn, were thrilled that he had prepared for us a hot fish chowder with the cod that I had caught that morning. It helped warm our chilled bodies and cheer our despondent spirits. The ship was water drenched and cold when we proceeded, under power, to a good anchorage spot on the east side of Codroy Island. At 8:30 PM, Charlie, John, and Marilyn went ashore in hopes of getting a full drum of gasoline. I stayed on board with Peggy, who had been sick all day. They came back with a few more groceries and the news that the place was closed and we couldn't get the gas until morning. It was apparent that we were all exhausted from going around in circles during the long, frustrating day, so we all retired early.

Day 22: August 12, 1953, Wednesday
At Anchor — Codroy Island, Newfoundland

Everyone had arisen from their wet bunks, still dressed in damp clothes, by 8:30 AM only to find another foggy, wet day awaiting and not a breath of wind. The good news was that we were not far from Port aux Basques, a very important port in our remaining itinerary, and we would soon be able to purchase a good supply of gasoline. A breakfast of *hot* cocoa, toast, and juice got our individual *human* engines off to a good start for the new day.

John and Charlie went ashore in the dinghy to Codroy to purchase the all-important gasoline. They soon returned, jubilantly towing a 350-pound drum of gasoline in the water behind rodney. We all were needed to hoist that heavy baby up on the deck.

Once it was soundly secured, they filled the starboard and port tanks with the precious gas. It took them some time to get the old, tired, and temperamental engine to purr again; it was 2:30 PM before we took off from our mooring. In a light northwest breeze, we raised the mizzen and main only to have the wind drop when we were abeam Shag Ledge at 4:20 PM. We lowered the sails and proceeded by motor to Red Rock Point where the rains pelted down and the dense fog moved in. The visibility was down to two hundred yards and sometimes only one hundred. John stood on the bow with a heavy-duty flashlight watching for shoals and cliffs as we inched forward as slowly as we could.

Finally, at 5:00 PM, the fog lifted and we were in the clear to run free, and we raised the mizzen. With the help of the motor, we were abeam the Port aux Basques light at 6:15 PM and tied up to the CNS dock at 7:00 PM.

We all went ashore to the Twin Towns Inn and had a dinner of Newfoundland rabbit. Perhaps any hot meal would have evoked the same delightful reaction, but this one in particular tasted heavenly.

Peggy didn't fly from Stephenville after all and will be staying at this inn tonight, leaving on the SS *Cabot Strait* tomorrow, which we expect will be berthed right here beside us before morning.

At the inn, the men took advantage of the facilities to wash and shave for the first time in three days. Marilyn and I were even more resourceful. When we found that the upstairs ladies room contained a bathtub, we couldn't resist. Each of us took a bath and shampoo and used the wonderful dry, fluffy towels that just happened to be there.

Upon arrival in Port aux Basques, we had called our friend Phyllis Stevens, wife of Allan, the Royal Mounted policeman we had known in St. Anthony. We were pleased to hear her voice and to know that she would pay us a visit tomorrow.

The crew was in a happy frame of mind when we all returned to our ship. We had cleaned up, had a wonderful dinner, the *Northern Messenger* had plenty of gas and water, so we sat up to play bridge until we could get the 12:30 AM weather forecast. It didn't sound very promising. Our next run will be across the sixty or seventy miles of the Cabot Strait to Cape Breton, Nova Scotia. We'll all be greatly relieved when we have reached those shores.

Day 23: August 13, 1953, Thursday
CNS Dock — Port aux Basques, Newfoundland

On this morning, there is dense fog with visibility of only a half mile. We have too many things scheduled to be able to sail, so hopefully the fog will dissipate during the day.

We were enjoying a leisurely breakfast of oatmeal, Spam, French toast, corn bread, and cocoa when we heard a tap on the hatch cover. A Royal Mounted policeman appeared in all his regalia. His mission had been to find us and check on the condition of the ship and crew. We had been reported as missing by the Coast Guard since the third of August . We assured him that we were all okay but had experienced a "bit of engine trouble."

The following excerpts appeared in newspaper articles in Newfoundland:

U.S. SHIP IS MISSING OFF WEST COAST

Sgt. Keough of the local detachment of the R.C.M.P. reported this morning that word had been received from the U.S. Coast Guard at Argentia that *The Northern Messenger* with a crew of four *sic* on board, had left Bonne Bay on August 3rd and has been unheard from since.

The vessel, with a green hull and white trimming on top, was to have called in at Port aux Basques, Corner Brook, and North Sydney.

Mrs. Charles Terry *sic* of Massachusetts and wife of one of the crew members, reported the matter to the Coast Guard. Her husband was to have wired her from each port of call. The ship is due in the States on August 19th.

Any person having information as to the whereabouts of the ship are asked to contact the R.M.C.P here immediately.

ENGINE TROUBLE DELAYS ARRIVAL OF VESSEL. The *Northern Messenger*, reported as missing by the U.S. Coast Guard at Argentia yesterday, turned up later in the day at Port aux Basques.

When the ship pulled into Port aux Basques yesterday, the crew advised local officials there that they had encountered some engine trouble which resulted in being thrown off schedule.

We said our good-byes to Peggy. John accompanied her to the *Cabot Strait*, bag and baggage. Charlie had customs business to do, and Marilyn and I worked on scrubbing the decks and filling the water tanks. Later, the men disassembled the engine, putting in a new gasket, and cleaning the carburetor and sparkplugs.

In the afternoon, Phyllis Stevens arrived, and we all went ashore with her to pick up groceries and to send telegrams. We spent the evening at the Stevens home and were treated to a great dinner. We were back at the dock in time to see a smiling Peggy and her ship depart, and we all waved good-bye as she stood on the solid deck of the *Cabot Strait*.

When we all retired at 1:00 AM after chatting about the day's events and our plans for the next day, we were aware of the still dense fog bank. The visibility was barely fifty feet. This did not bode well for an early departure tomorrow.

Day 24: August 14, 1953, Friday
CNS Dock —Port aux Basques, Newfoundland

The fog was still with us delaying our departure until it finally lifted. While we were enjoying a leisurely breakfast of bacon, eggs, oatmeal, toast, and coffee, we heard another tap on the hatch cover. This time, a messenger brought a telegram to Charlie from his wife, Norma, in Boston simply saying, *Would like to know what you think you are doing!* We later learned that Norma had not received any word from Charlie since Bonne Bay and, in desperation, had contacted the Coast Guard. The message that was supposed to have been sent by Ann from Corner Brook was never received. Norma had expected our arrival in Boston by July 31.

The Newfoundland newspapers had been contacted and published an article—"U.S. Coast Guard Ship is Missing Off West Coast." They got their facts mixed up a bit and also spelled Charlie's name incorrectly (Terry instead of Currie).

Norma's telegram precipitated much soul-searching for poor Charlie and no doubt he was thinking, *Should I abandon my dream of mooring the* Northern Messenger *in Boston Harbor in order to get home quickly to my forlorn, concerned, pregnant and justifiably disgusted, wife?*

Much discussion took place by the crew. With several deadlines approaching, it was apparent that the crew would be dwindling soon— John to medical school, and I back to St. Anthony. Charlie came to the conclusion that the cons were outweighing the pros, by far, and made the decision to cross over to Cape Breton today, then sail down that beautiful coastline to North Sydney, Nova Scotia, and place the *Northern Messenger* in storage. Each of the members of the crew would then depart, scattering in four different directions. We were relieved that now we had a definite plan and we were nearing our new destination.

The weather forecast for the day was glum—"storm warnings to small crafts along the Nova Scotia coast." It seems that this season, the Gulf of St. Lawrence received the tail end of gale-force winds of hurricanes that hit the eastern Atlantic coast, and it seemed to us that they had found the *Northern Messenger* most of the time.

In spite of the forecast, we spent the afternoon getting the ship ready to sail. The men got the engine all tuned up, and it was running smoothly. After a fruit salad supper prepared by Marilyn, we decided to make a dash for Cape North (on Cape Breton, Nova Scotia) some sixty plus miles away.

We left the dock at 5:55 PM, and after clearing the harbour buoys, we set our course for 250 degrees magnetic. Visibility was one mile, and there was a slight swell in the ocean. As we sailed throughout the night, John and Marilyn took the first watch. During that time, the fog did lift and the night became clear with a mild southwest wind of five miles per hour. Charlie and I took over the helm at midnight.

Swordfishing Boat on Cabot Strait (RML)

Day 25: August 15, 1953, Saturday
At Sea— Crossing the Cabot Strait

At 2:30 AM, we heard that old familiar sputtering sound from the engine, and then—yes—it died. This time, the coil was short-circuiting, and there was water in the cylinder and carburetor. We hoisted the mainsail, mizzen, and working jib and moved along at a pretty good rate with no land in sight yet. We could see beautiful phosphorescent bubbles trailing behind us in the wake of the ship. At 6:00 AM Marilyn and John took over the watch to allow us to get some rest.

When I awoke at 10:00 AM, Cape Breton was visible in the distance through the fog; the skies looked ominous. At 11:00 AM, we saw several vessels—a Trans-Caribbean motor vessel of eight thousand tons, a couple of boats containing ores, and a small fleet of swordfishing boats. The harpooner was on the bowsprit and the lookout men way up in the crow's nest. We wanted to go south to Ingonish, but with a storm on the horizon, we had to head for Neil's Cove, whose foghorn we could hear loud and clear. We were thankful to find a wharf where we tied up at 12:15 PM. We had just barely finished securing the lines and breathed joint sighs of relief when we were approached by several local sailors with the warning that southeast gale winds were in the forecast, and they gave us this admonition: "You can't stay in here. This is a poor harbour in a southeast storm. The waves bounce off the cliffs and then roll back. *Your boat will be hammered against the dock, and you'll lose it!*" Such an upsetting greeting to a crew who thought that, at last, they were out of harm's way.

By this time, we were all being drenched as the rains pelted down. We scurried to prepare for a quick departure to a safer harbour. Marilyn and I fastened down the deck equipment even more strongly, pumped the bilge, while the men and a local mechanic worked on the engine.

By 3:00 PM, the sea had really built up, and we were being beaten against the dock just as the men had said. It was still pouring rain, and the wind was twenty miles per hour. There were many dire predictions from the crowd of onlookers on the dock that we'd never make it out of the harbour.

At 3:45 PM, without the benefit of an engine, we cast off, raised the mainsail, and made four tacks into the wind to get out of the harbour. Because of the fury of the wind and its direction, we had to head for Dingwall, twenty miles to the *north* instead of south to Ingonish as we had planned. The gloomy crowd from the dock had gathered at the mouth of the harbour by the lighthouse in anticipation of a shipwreck.

On that last tack, I was kneeling by the main sheet when John accidentally took the stop off the mainsail. We jibed unexpectedly, and as the boom swung over with a thud, I was hit by the block and knocked down. My head and arm banged on the deck. The arm swelled up, and I was afraid it might be broken, but it soon was in working order again. (The head seemed to work okay also.) I was very lucky not to have been hit by the heavy boom.

We made it to Dingwall in record time, sailing with the wind all the time. We arrived at 5:40 PM and tied up to a Toronto dredge, *McNamara*, since there were no empty slips. All the ships had stayed in port that day. The rain was pounding down while we furled the sails. The friendly sailors on the dredge gave us hot tea and insisted that we bring over our wet clothing to dry in their warm engine room. Just like in Newfoundland, we found great hospitality and assistance. "The ship *really* is soaked this time," reads my log.

Not to waste an opportunity for enjoying local color, Marilyn and John found a country dance scheduled for the evening and reported back to us at midnight that they had a great time.

Day 26: August 16, 1953, Sunday
Tied to Dredge— Dingwall, Cape Breton, Nova Scotia

We could tell, even from our bunks, that the wind was still raging, so everyone slept until 9:00 AM, knowing there was no sailing out into Cape North with this kind of weather.

After a late breakfast, we welcomed the opportunity to explore this beautiful Cape Breton area, which is such an ideal location along the Cabot Trail. We observed the swordfish boats at close range and talked with many of the restless crew members who were anxious to get out to the sea to do their fishing.

For lunch, we found a canteen where we could get ham and cheese sandwiches, hotdogs, milk shakes, Cokes, and sundaes. After such a long time without them, they tasted "some good."

We spent the rest of the day drying out the boat and our belongings and general tidying up. *Oh,* I forgot—and Charlie and John worked on the engine.

I prepared the supper of creamed salmon and baked potatoes and fried some kind of batter left from breakfast. (John's log reads: "Rosie's buns would not rise.")

After playing a few hands of bridge, we retired early, feeling certain we would be sailing *south* tomorrow.

Day 27: August 17, 1953, Monday
Tied to Dredge— Dingwall, Cape Breton, Nova Scotia

We were awakened at 4:45 AM by a shout from the captain of the *McNamara* with the report that they were about to leave. There was a light southwest wind, the rain had stopped, and the sky was clear, except for thousands of brilliant stars. We decided that we would move out also, after clearing the decks of all loose paraphernalia.

At 5:00 AM, we were ready to head south to Ingonish or perhaps all the way to North Sydney if the wind would only cooperate. We cast off the lines, raised the mizzen, mainsail, and jib. There was a beautiful sunrise at 6:05 AM, and we had nice, smooth sailing after we moved out of Aspy Bay. We were abeam Ingonish by noon where we hit a rainsquall, and the high wind caused the mizzen throat halyard to break, dropping the sail. We were taking on a lot of water through the broken hawsepipe (from *the* storm) requiring us to pump the bilge four times that morning. Charlie opted not to attempt the run to North Sydney but rather to head in for Ingonish. This required tacking many times with the very erratic wind; first it would be fifteen to twenty miles per hour, then it would be absolutely flat. This went on for hours until the crew of a swordfishing boat understood our predicament and came to the rescue and offered to tow us in. The *Wesley Keith* towed us in through the tickle to the area where the fishing fleet was, and we moored at 6:00 PM. The harbour was beautiful but tight, filled with swordfish boats. This was our first reminder of the sights and sounds of a horde of raucous tourists. We knew we had left behind the charm and tranquility of the small fishing villages of Newfoundland where, during the summer months, there was almost no transportation to anywhere except by boat.

After our supper onboard, we all walked and explored the surrounding area; Charlie found a pay phone and called his wife in Boston. Norma was greatly relieved to hear his voice and all was forgiven. She was happy to learn of his decision to store the boat in North Sydney and that our destination was only about *thirty-five miles away!*

Nearing the end of our trip, we were all anxious to get started on the last leg in the morning. I was especially concerned because I learned that the *Burgeo* would be leaving on the nineteenth at 9:30 PM from North Sydney to cross the Cabot Strait. That would be my only possible connection with the coastal steamer, *Springdale*, in Port aux Basques, that would transport me back to St. Anthony.

Day 28: August 18, 1953, Tuesday
Moored — Ingonish, Cape Breton, Nova Scotia

We shipmates were calm, trying to remain cheerful and optimistic, while at the same time realizing how essential it was for us to reach North Sydney by August 18 (*today*) or at the very latest *tomorrow*. We are so near to that elusive goal—*just thirty-five miles.*

We awoke to a clear, beautiful day but with no wind. This would have been fine if we had had a dependable engine that would cooperate just for those last few miles. Charlie has spent hours working on the current problem. One of the local mechanics has diagnosed the situation. "A bad manifold in the number 4 cylinder and too much water pressure is forcing water back into the engine." Charlie also had discovered two broken valve springs. He found a fellow in town who also owns a Gray (marine engine) and was able to pick up two springs from him.

Marilyn and John took the opportunity in the morning to go to the beach for relaxation. We all were pleased to be invited to go with Dr. Dunfey and his wife to see the Keltic Lodge. They drove us, in the afternoon, to the legendary place located on a high bluff overlooking the bay and ocean beyond, right on the popular Cabot Trail. Except for the fact that we absolutely must reach North Sydney tomorrow, this would have been a lovely area to explore and enjoy for a while. We were too preoccupied with completing this last leg of our journey to fully appreciate the beauties of Cape Breton.

Our food larder was becoming bare. Our last supper (we hoped) consisted of the many surprises that were in the remaining cans that were previously unidentified. We were barely aware of what we were eating with our thoughts and efforts on other things, such as packing and getting the ship ready for storage.

We hit the bunks early so that we would be ready to depart in the morning. We chatted about having a celebration dinner in North Sydney at some nice restaurant. We fantasized about the menu; lobster was a popular choice along with *plenty of ice cream!*

Day 29: August 19, 1953, Wednesday
Moored — Ingonish, Cape Breton, Nova Scotia

This is the critical day. Charlie was up early, and we could hear the engine running. What a fantastic melodic sound that was.

We had a little more packing to do, messages to be sent from shore, and small jobs on the ship; and by 11:00 AM, we were ready to sail. Charlie revved up the engine, we cast off the lines, but the ship would not budge; *we were aground!* It was low tide, and now we must wait for the tide to come in and float us out of this cove. It was very significant that our very *last* obstacle (we thought *then*) had nothing to do with our fickle engine but rather of one of the profound powers of nature that has flowed rhythmically and predictably since the earth was formed—*the tide.*

Finally at 1:30 PM, we were finally afloat. We were ready to cast off again. Believe it or not, the engine *would not start.* Charlie patiently took off the carburetor, drained the water, and dried the spark plugs. This time when he tried to start her up, there was a new awful growling sound—*the battery was dead!* John went ashore and was able to borrow a battery from one of the swordfish boats, and Charlie and John used their magic to get the engine started by 2:30 PM.

We finally motored out of the harbour and set our course for North Sydney. We were moving along really well for the first ten miles when the engine suddenly sputtered and stopped. The boost from the borrowed battery was enough to start the engine but apparently not enough to keep it going. Our battery was *dead.* That sputtering was the very last sound that I ever heard from that engine.

Just as we were beginning to doubt that we could catch the *Burgeo* in time, a miraculous stiff breeze came up. The sea was calm and flat, and we just tore down the coastline with each and every sail filled. It was a beautiful sight. Those were the very best sailing conditions of the entire twenty-nine days, and we were elated!

This turn of events made us feel as if we were being rewarded for the countless hours of misery dealing with the engine problems, the gale-force winds—which were not typical of this season—and the other trials and tribulations that we had endured. It had tested our mettle and created a strong bond among the four of us.

We reached North Sydney and tied up at the Warehouse Pier at 9:10 PM. The *Burgeo* was still there, but the horn was blasting; she was all set to depart. I grabbed my bags, said a hurried good-bye to my friends, and ran to the telegraph office. When I finally reached the *Burgeo*, the crew was just pulling up the gangplank; I was the last one to board the ship, which left *on time* at exactly 9:30 PM. From the deck, I waved farewell to my fellow shipmates and wished there had been time to express how much their friendship had meant to me. I was sadly aware that I might never see any of them again.

As the *Burgeo* pulled out past the *Northern Messenger*, I waved good-bye to her too. She had been a noble friend, taking us safely through storms of which we (and perhaps she) had never seen the likes. I almost could hear her proudly exclaiming, "I got you all here on time after all, didn't I? I'm really a sailing vessel. We could have done it without that engine."

As the *Burgeo* moved further out of the harbour, I mused, *"We never did have that lobster dinner celebration in North Sydney."*

August 20–24, 1953
Return Trip From North Sydney, Nova Scotia
To St. Anthony, Newfoundland

I disembarked from the *Burgeo* the next morning after leaving my friends in North Sydney. My next leg required taking the Newfoundland Railway from Port aux Basques to Corner Brook where I would connect, hopefully, with the coastal steamer, *Springdale*. (This was the same railroad line that had the wreck on my initial trip to St. Anthony in 1952.) The train ride this time was uneventful, except for the scare I had at the first stop. While I got off to make an important phone call, within minutes, the train pulled away from the station; I dropped the phone in the middle of the conversation and ran, catching up to the last car. The conductor was standing in the doorway, and I grabbed his outstretched hand, and he pulled me aboard.

SS Springdale, *coastal steamer*
(*Courtesy of Railway Coastal Museum, St. John's*)

Upon arrival in Corner Brook, we saw the *Springdale* tied up to the wharf with the freight already loaded; the captain was just waiting for the passengers from this specific train. I barely had time to board and get situated in my cabin before the horn blared, and we were *off*.

I enjoyed the unaccustomed luxury of being served a nice hot meal before walking in the long corridor, without any fear of falling, to my warm, dry cabin where a normal-sized bunk awaited me, already outfitted with clean white sheets. The ship barely rolled, and it was hard to tell that we were traveling up the same coast that we so recently had sailed down. In the morning, I was invited by the captain to come to the bridge to see a demonstration of their navigational system. I was amazed at all of the modern equipment, compared to our parallel rule and dividers, outdated charts, AM portable radio, and the chip log that John let trail behind the ship. The *Springdale*'s speed was about twelve knots compared to our ship's seven knots (under the best of conditions).

It was interesting to watch the freight being unloaded at the various ports. There were many kinds of pulleys and winches, even a sling that offloaded a horse. We certainly would have welcomed that device to get that 350-pound gasoline drum on board the *Northern Messenger*.

On the second day, we were at St. Barbe (near Current Island where we had been storm-bound for five days). We were delayed at Flower's Cove waiting for the sea to calm down. The wind posed no problem for our ship, but the small boats were bouncing up and down, unable to handle the freight from the anchored *Springdale*.

On the third day, we crossed the Straits of Belle Isle and were at Forteau in just a few hours. I was reminded of our crossing on July 26 (from the opposite direction) in that storm that took us in to Current Island. Lesley Diack, from the nursing station, came onboard during the brief stop to say hello and hear about our "trip to Boston." She was relieved to learn that we had survived the trip.

By the next morning, we were at Battle Harbour on the Labrador, farther north than I had previously traveled. We left there at 10:30 the next morning with one more stop at Raleigh at 4:45 PM and then across the northern peninsula of Newfoundland where we had sailed on that first day on the *Northern Messenger*.

Upon arrival in St. Anthony that evening, I realized that I had experienced something special during those twenty-nine days. I was to have many other adventures during my two years in St. Anthony and my sixty-one years since, but now at age eighty-seven, I recognize that the voyage on the *Northern Messenger* was, indeed, *the greatest adventure of all.*

Epilogue

My attempts to find the present location of the crew members of the *Northern Messenger* have been lengthy, convoluted, and at times, discouraging. Marilyn and I were reunited in 2007, when she was in Florida to visit her daughter. The long search for Charlie was finally ended only a few weeks ago when I actually talked with him. I still have not been able to find Peggy Armstrong.

Charles Currie, our captain, arrived home safely to Boston in time for the birth of his daughter—with less than two weeks to spare! He then held engineering positions in the Boston area and later in Rochester, New York. He and his wife, Norma, had two children—Susan N. (Currie) Price and John C. Currie—and four grandchildren. Norma died in 2006. Charlie, now age eighty-seven, is retired and lives in Rochester, New York. He enjoys his hobbies of woodworking, woodcarving, and golf and being near his family.

Charles Currie (JC)

John C. Jenkins was from New Glasgow, Nova Scotia. He graduated from medical school at Dalhousie, Nova Scotia, in 1958 and became a practicing physician until 1964 and then specialized in anesthesiology. In retirement, he continued his interest in the sea and sailed extensively. John died in 2007 at the age of seventy-nine.

John Jenkins (JJ)

Marilyn Tolley Jenkins married John Jenkins in 1954 while he was in medical school. They had six children during their life together—John, Ellen, Carol, Rebecca, Lucia, and Ruth. Marilyn, now age eighty-four, is enjoying living at Christie Gardens in Toronto, Canada. She sings in the chorus, plays her clarinet, and remains active.

Marilyn (Tolley) Jenkins (LJ)

Peggy Armstrong has been among the missing. All attempts to locate her have been to no avail. I assume that she is in the Toronto, Canada, area. If she should read this, I hope she will contact me.

Rosalie Lombard returned to St. Anthony for the following year. She then returned to Columbia-Presbyterian (her alma mater) and taught medical-surgical nursing. Her interest in sailing, acquired on the voyage of the *Northern Messenger*, continued; and while living in Burlington, Vermont, she purchased a twenty-six-foot Pearson, which she sailed for years with friends on Lake Champlain. She continued her career primarily in nursing education and nursing administration. She is now retired and living at The Villages in Florida, where at age eighty-seven, she is still healthy and active.

Rosalie Lombard (RML)

The *Northern Messenger* remained in North Sydney, Nova Scotia, under new ownership for an unknown period of time. Then, presumably, she was sailed from North Sydney through the St. Peter's Canal and moored in Strachan's Cove in the Bras d'Or Lake, where she unfortunately sank some years later. John visited the site in 1975 with some of his family and engaged a friend to dive down and check out the remains. The ship was pretty well deteriorated, but he brought up an anchor hawser and an unknown piece of brass tubing as mementos of that voyage on the *Northern Messenger* twenty-one years earlier. It is of some comfort to know that the ship found her final days in the spectacular surroundings in Cape Breton on Bras d'Or Lake, which means the "arms of gold."

Afterthoughts—2014

These experiences occurred over sixty-two years ago. It is unbelievable to me now that the span of years is so great because some of the memories are just as vivid today as the events were then. Upon my return from Newfoundland and Labrador, my life became very busy with a career in nursing, educational pursuits, travel, and other enriching experiences.

During the past five to ten years, my thoughts have increasingly turned to the time that I spent in St. Anthony and the realization that those experiences were truly unique. When I gathered my memorabilia, it consisted of movies, letters, notes, my *Northern Messenger* log, special mementos (such as carvings and embroidery)—all of which inspired me to start writing about some of the events from those bygone years.

I have kept abreast of the events that have shaped the tremendous changes that have occurred in Newfoundland and Labrador. Certainly, the discovery of the Viking settlement in 1960 at L'Anse aux Meadows, and its subsequent impact on the tourist industry, was a major incentive to provide access to the site. As roads were added and airplane travel became more prevalent, major changes occurred in St. Anthony and elsewhere.

Following confederation in 1949, the increasing interest in and financial assistance to its latest province, Canada has had a profound effect on the progression of events leading to northern Newfoundland and Labrador's present state of affairs.

Grenfell's vision is now being realized. Gone is the patriarchal role of the Grenfell Mission, but it left the realization that northern

Newfoundland and Labrador are so much more enhanced because of those early years; without which the present system could not have flourished. Ironically, it involved a transition in which the International Grenfell Association gradually relinquished its role in the region as a voluntary charitable organization, and as of 1984, control was in the hands of the provincial government. Today's health care system is the Labrador-Grenfell Regional Authority (Labrador-Grenfell Health), formed in 2005, providing care to around 37,000 people, with 1,557 staff members and twenty-two facilities. Its website reports that it provides the following services: acute care, diagnostic and clinical support, community health and wellness, dental, health protection, long-term care, mental health and addictions, residential, and therapeutic intervention, family rehabilitation, and other rehabilitation services.

I have relived many of the memories during the process of writing this book. Although it was just a two-year slice out of my eighty-seven years, it has had a profound impact. I met so many wonderful patients, some of whom I shared a critical time in their lives. I will always remember and hopefully be able to emulate, the patience, grace, and generosity that were so characteristic of the Newfoundland-Labrador people. I was privileged to work with professional people from many other cultures who served their time up north with that same spirit, which Sir Wilfred Grenfell expressed in these words: "The purpose of the world is not to have and hold, but to serve." It is a testament to Grenfell's great impact on its history that the website for Labrador-Health still prominently displays these same words.

Curtis Hospital in St. Anthony—today
(Courtesy of Labrador-Grenfell Health)

Bibliography

Cairis, Nicholas T. *Era of the Passenger Liner*. San Francisco, Ca.: Argonaut Books, 1992.

Cook, Clayton D. *Tales of the Rails: The Newfoundland Railway 1881–1988*. St. John's: Flanker Press Ltd., 2005.

Diack, Lesley. *Labrador Nurse*. London: Victor Gollancz, 1963.

Grenfell, Wilfred T. *Forty Years for Labrador*. Boston and New York: Houghton Mifflin Company, 1932.

Jenkins, John C. *Personal Log from the Northern Messenger Trip*. 1953.

Johansen, Michael. *Moon Spotlight Newfoundland and Labrador*. Berkeley, Ca.: Avalon Travel, Perseus Books Group, 2011.

Jupp, Dorothy M. *A Journey of Wonder and Other Writings*. New York: Vantage, 1971.

Loder, Millicent Blake. *Daughter of Labrador*. St. John's: Harry Cuff, 1989.

Lombard, Rosalie M. *Personal Log from the Northern Messenger Trip*. 1953.

Mowat, Farley. *The New Founde Land*. Toronto: McClelland & Stewart, 1989.

O'Brien, Patricia. *The Grenfell Obsession: An Anthology*. St. John's: Creative Publishers, 1992.

Paddon, W. A. Labrador Doctor: *My Life with the Grenfell Mission*. James Lorimer & Company, 1989.

Patey, Francis. *The Grenfell Dock*. St. Anthony: Bebb Publishing, 1993.

Rompkey, Ronald, ed. *Jessie Luther at the Grenfell Mission*. McGill-Queen's University Press, 2001.

Smallwood, Joseph R. *Encyclopedia of Newfoundland and Labrador*. Newfoundland Book Publishers Ltd. 1981.

Stevens, James P. *Reminiscences of a Boothbay Shipbuilder*. Boothbay Region Historical Society, 1993.

Thomas, Gordon W. *From Sled to Satellite: My Years with the Grenfell Mission*. Toronto: Irwin Publishing, 1987.

Toland, Harry. *A Sort of Peace Corps*. Maryland: Heritage Books Inc., 2001.

Walls, Martha. *Newfoundland and Labrador Book of Everything*. Lunenburg, Nova Scotia: MacIntyre Purcell Publishing Inc., 2012.

Acknowledgments

This book was launched by the urgings of friends and relatives who either saw my movie, read my letters, or heard of my adventures in Newfoundland and Labrador. During these many years since, they have encouraged me to write them down. My efforts at writing have been spasmodic when other events or responsibilities pushed to the forefront. I have had the benefit of quite a collection of books and memorabilia to aid in my recollections, but my memory has played the major role. This past year, I have felt an urgency to finish the book while I am active, healthy, and with memory fairly well intact.

I appreciate the persistent prodding of my good friend from student-nursing days, Betty Hanway. I owe her thanks for the gentle but ever present reminder to *keep writing*. Other friends and relatives have given encouragement and their critiques, but my friend, Joanne McClellan, read and reread ad infinitum and offered suggestions. I thank her for her patience.

I owe a huge debt of gratitude to my friend in St. Anthony, Agnes Patey. She has always been interested and involved in the Grenfell experience, starting with her early years as a patient in the St. Anthony hospital. Having held many prominent positions in the general office, the finance office, the Grenfell Historical Society, and the Grenfell Foundation, she has a veritable treasure trove of all information Grenfell.

When she hasn't had the answer to my multitude of questions, she either set out to find it or put me in contact with the right source.

During the past few months of more intensive concentration, I have had help and cooperation from the families of my *Northern Messenger* crew members. In particular, Lucia Jenkins has gathered helpful information from her siblings as well as making available to me the log, which her father kept on our trip. It was priceless in enabling me to correlate events with the benefit of two different perspectives. The same can be said for Charles Currie's son, John, and daughter-in-law, Alison.

Paul Rabenold has done a yeoman's job of unlocking still photos from my eight-millimeter movie film of sixty-two years ago, and I appreciate his computer expertise and patience.

Last, but certainly not least, has been the invaluable assistance from Mary Zdan in typing and formatting the materials for the final submission to the publisher. She has provided the key momentum that helped me to stay focused, and I thank her for her patience and optimistic demeanor.

My greatest thanks go to the patients, staff, and Newfoundlanders, whom I was privileged to know, and for their individual contributions to a most significant period in my life.

About the Author

ROSALIE M. LOMBARD spent most of her career in some aspect of nursing. Following her two years in St. Anthony, she taught nursing at Columbia University and the University of Vermont, where she was an associate professor. She later was the associate director of nursing at the Medical Center Hospital of Vermont. Her academic degrees are from Columbia University, Teachers College Columbia University, and Boston University.

In retirement she lives in The Villages, Florida. She would welcome communication from anyone with a special interest in the Grenfell era in Newfoundland and Labrador. Her email address is RMLOM57@comcast

I shall be telling this with a sigh
Somewhere ages and ages hence:
Two roads diverged in a wood, and I—
I took the one less traveled by.
And that has made all the difference.

—Robert Frost

Made in the USA
San Bernardino, CA
22 March 2015